THE UGLY BLACK BIRD

Joanna Siedlecka

Translated from the Polish by Chester A. Kisiel

This book has been published with the support of the Polish Book Institute.

Cover designed by Lyndsay Ream

This book is a work of historical fact. Names, characters, places exist or existed, and incidents really happened.

Original Polish language edition copyright © by Joanna Siedlecka

First Edition in English: Dec 2018
Leopolis Press

ISBN- 978-1-7335238-0-6

"... This is the most powerful joint-venture in history. These two diasporas -- the Catholic, Polish diaspora and the Jewish diaspora -- have a common denominator, which forms a community of the closest ties.... We shall never part."

- Jerzy Kosiński

(Passage from a lecture "Divided Presence" -- September 1990, Jagiellonian University)

Contents

Prologue

The Ugly Black Bird (Marabut and Cis, Warsaw-Gdańsk, 1994) by Joanna Siedlecka is a book about the wartime childhood of Jerzy Kosiński that explodes yet another mystification of the Great Mystifier. For, the truth was entirely different from what he presented in his biographies; for instance, Current Biography speaks of the supposedly autobiographic *The Painted Bird* - the author's "wandering alone through Eastern Europe," "cruelties and violence," "loss of speech."

The Ugly Black Bird is based on the accounts of still-living witnesses of those days, who describe the true wartime history of Kosiński. To be precise, the history of the Lewinkopf-Kosińskis, who survived the occupation quietly and safely thanks to simple Polish people of the provinces. First in Sandomierz, a little town of a few thousand, then in the nearby village of Dąbrowa Rzczecyka, which today is in Tarnobrzeg province. The Kosińskis did not hide, they carried Aryan papers and, considering that it was the occupation, lived in better than decent conditions. They rented a two-room furnished apartment in the village, bought expensive food, had a maid. "Old man" Kosiński, who unlike his wife and son, had a "passable" appearance, worked in the state purchasing center, gave lessons, engaged in politics - he had connections with the local "red" partisans.

The Kosińskis experienced no cruelties. On the contrary, they experienced help and kindness. The peasants obviously knew that they were Jews, but - despite the well-known consequences - it never entered anyone's mind to denounce them to the Germans stationed nearby. The village was poor, backward, illiterate, but decent, deeply religious, understanding that "these are also people and want to live."

In the spring of 1945 the Kosińskis left Dąbrowa and all contact with them was lost. Neither "old man" Kosiński nor "young" Kosiński sent any news, did not write a single word. When Jerzy Kosiński came to Poland in the spring of 1989, his old acquaintances went to Warsaw to see him. Perhaps he didn't remember the name of the village, they thought, but he received them coldly, got rid of them by promising to write, to visit them. They felt even more offended when they read *The Painted Bird*. In it they found Dąbrowa - the same landscapes, places, situations, first names, last names. Everything, except the cruelties.

So, The Ugly Black Bird is also the story of those to whom Jerzy Kosiński owed his survival. It is about their drama, pain, bitterness. It is also about an author's moral responsibility for creating his autobiography.

Translation

CHESTER A. KISIEL was born in the United States, where he received degrees from Brown, Harvard, and the University of Chicago. He now resides in Warsaw and works as a translator. His translations for Polish and foreign publishers include books in philosophy, art, economics, sociology, and history, among them Janusz Tazbir's *Poland as the Rampart of Christian Europe,* Szymon Laks's *Music of Another World,* Jozef Banka's *An Open Ontology,* Jadwiga Staniszkis's *The Dynamics of the Breakthrough in Eastern Europe,* W. Tatarkiewicz's *History of Philosophy* and *History of Aesthetics,* and M. Kalecki's *Capitalism: Business Cycles and Full Employment.*

Notes from the Author

I did not go to America. I did not want to write about Jerzy Kosiński's unquestionably stunning career or about his scandals, successes and distinctions, which have already been written about by others.

I was interested solely in his wartime childhood. A trip to the places where, as a young boy, he lived through the occupation. For, in my opinion, his experiences from those years, his traumatic childhood, and not America, are the key to his real nature, to his mysterious, complicated, "Holocaust dominated" personality. To his obsessions, phobias, animosities and apprehensions. To his masks and mystifications. To shocking prose permeated by an obsession with evil. And finally-- to his death by suicide, among who's not fully explained reasons, some people have also included his "bleak childhood," which, with its ghosts of the past, from which he was unable to free himself, kept coming back to haunt him.

"He was a great mystifier" -- Janusz Głowacki wrote of him – "but the demons whose presence he always felt behind his back were real. On one certain night they closed in on him in the apartment on 57th Street."[1*]

"... I think that the years of childhood described in *The Painted Bird* also had an influence on the decision to take his own life. Even if this childhood was not as terrible as described in the novel" -- said Ewa Hoffman, a Canadian writer of Polish origin, authoress of a book on the adaptation of Polish emigrants in the U.S.A."[**]

The "bleak childhood" is also the key to *The Painted Bird*, which is recognized as a literary masterpiece of the Holocaust, its literary document.

Though Kosiński emphasized the universality of the novel, none-the-less - like most of his works, which he called "self-fiction" -- the story stirred up questions

---

[*] *Jerzy Kosinsl.i. Twarz i Maski,* Museum of Art - Łódź, Reprint, Warsaw 1992

[**] "Gazeta Pomorska," No. 125, 31 May. 1991.

about its authenticity. People wondered: Is the author telling his own story? After all, he was a Jewish child who survived the Age of the Ovens.

The more so as in his official "biographies" published in American literary encyclopedias he gave facts consistent with the story of the Boy from *The Painted Bird*. For example, according to Current Biography - he -- like the Boy – "was sent during the war to the countryside," "separated from the person to whom he had been entrusted." "He wandered from village to village," stigmatized on account of his swarthy countenance, "magnetic hair," "persecuted by fair-skinned and fair-haired villagers, he suffered many physical and mental horrors, as a result of which he lost the power of speech for five years." Contemporary Authors writes – "abandoned, hungry, he wandered under the continual suspicion that he was a Jewish or a Gypsy child."

The album Jerzy Kosiński. Twarz i Maski -- the only Polish biographical source -- also repeats this "biography": "In 1939 ... fearing for the life of their son, the parents sent him to a female acquaintance in the East, and they themselves were concealed by Poles in Łódź. After the war they found their son in an orphanage. He was mute on account of some traumatic experience from the time of the war. He regained his speech at the age of 15 ..."*

So, on the whole, the story of the Boy from the Bird was taken for Kosiński's own story, an impression which he often emphasized publicly and privately, stating that he had experienced all of the horrors that had befallen the Boy. Every incident is true - he admitted in Current Biography.

Elie Wiesel, who has devoted his entire life to the Holocaust, wrote an article about *The Painted Bird* for The New York Times. "I thought it was fiction" -- he said -- "but when he told me it was an autobiography, I tore up my article and wrote another one that was a thousand times better" ·

So, I have tried to re-create Kosiński's wartime history. My intention was not to "unmask" him, but to find out what had branded him so strongly for his entire life. And above all -- to discover the truth about his experiences during the occupation.

---

* *Jerzy Kosiński. Twarz I maski,* op. cit.

✻ ✻ ✻

It seems that he told no one, not even his friends, where and with whom he spent the war years. Nowhere did he ever write anything specific about this; he misled and camouflaged. So my task seemed hopeless. From the novel it is not even clear what country is the scene of the action, let alone what place.

According to Dictionary of Literary Biography— "he wandered through Poland and Russia," according to Current Biography – "through Eastern Europe, from village to village," while Contemporary Literary Criticism reports - "he spent the war in the Polish countryside."

On the other hand, in reviews, biographies, on jackets of Kosiński's books published in Poland, our critics spoke of his "wartime wandering life" on the "borderlands of the prewar Commonwealth," "Polish-Lithuanian-Belarus borderlands," "eastern borderlands," "the Ukraine," "Podlasie," "PolesieI," "Pinsk marshes," "the Vilnius region."

✻ ✻ ✻

Contrary to appearances, however, the re-creation of his wartime experiences unexpectedly turned out to be possible. I simply read <u>everything</u> that had ever been written about him, including the attacks, of course; and in the Kielce *Słowo Ludu* (No. 161/1968)[*] I hit upon an article that was more than critical, but, as itturned out, it contained the real names and addresses of persons with whom the Kosińskis had lived in the first years of the occupation. Thanks to this article, I tried to reconstruct the first, Sandomierz stage of their wartime fortunes.

I reconstructed the next stage thanks to the weekly Polityka, which in No.224/1982 and No. 10/1983 printed the letters of Andrzej Migdałek and Adam Latawiec, describing the next years of the occupation spent by the Kosiński family

---

[*] "Newsweek", 13 May 1991.

vi

in the village of Dąbrowa, commune of Radomyśl on the river San, province of Tarnobrzeg.

I went there with Mr. Migdałek and right away I knew that it was <u>that</u> village. Before one of the cottages covered with bird cages filled with birds, we were greeted by Lech the bird-fancier -- the local hair-brain, who still puts paint on birds and watches how their own flock later pecks them to death ...

The Ugly Black Bird unmasks yet another of the Famous Mystifier's mystifications. Perhaps the most important mystification, the one about his wartime biography, which, in a certain sense, was his calling card. For there was no "lonesome wandering life" through "Eastern Europe"; there were no "acts of physical barbarity and sadism."

Despite this, his own story, the story of the Lewinkopf-Kosińskis, who survived the occupation in a Polish village thanks to the peasants, a priest, and the local communist party cell, is, at least in my opinion, much more interesting. Deeper and more problematic. Exceptional and simply incredible.

My book is not only about Kosiński but also about the people to whom he owed his salvation; their drama is also worth recording

The Ugly Black Bird unquestionably touches upon the mystery of his "bleak childhood," perhaps even on one of the reasons for his suicide. Was he perhaps really ready to sacrifice his life to save his myth? The myth of one who had suffered the most?

And this time as well LIFE turned out to be stranger than fiction -- artificial, strained, overwhelming the reader mainly with sadism and atrocities.

Joanna Siedlecka

Chapter 1
Josek Lewinkopf, Zamkowa 8

Maria Lipinska of Zamkowa 8 in the center of Sandomierz, with whom the Kosińskis (at that time still the Lewinkopfs) stayed right after the outbreak of the war, when they fled from their native Łódź, is no longer living. But her children - Maria Wiktorowska (1917), retired school teacher of Sandomierz, Jan Lipiński (1922), farmer from nearby Mata Wies, and Tadeusz Lipiński (1920), now residing in Wroclaw -- remember them well.

They remember Moses Lewinkopf - the old man, as he seemed to them at that time, even though he was at most just over forty, but he was already balding, with a pot-belly. A rather Semitic type, but not so self-evident; in fact, he could have passed for a Pole or for a wealthy merchant or factory owner, in any case for a man of business, which he often emphasized in conversations. Intelligent, educated, fluent in several languages.

Elżbieta Lewinkopf, his wife, obviously younger than him, but also close to forty. Elegant, very pretty -- slim, taller than her husband, with clear Semitic looks: an aquiline nose, swarthy complexion, dark eyes and thick, curly hair.

Young Jerzy Lewinkopf was then around six years old and was a carbon copy of his mother, though even more Jewish-looking. An even more prominent nose, coal-black eyes, with a shock of raven-black hair. Very well cared for - clean as a whistle, beautifully dressed, speaking impeccable Polish. He was worshipped by his parents, who doted on their only child.

The Lewinkopfs arrived at the Lipińskis in the first months of the war with only a few valises. The Lipiński siblings think this was as early as October or November, but the official records show that the Lewinkopfs were not registered there until January 8. They came from Łódź, which had been incorporated into the German Reich; their beautiful spacious flat had been taken over by Germans.

In Sandomierz, which was in German occupied Poland, they thought they would be safer.

They were referred to Zamkowa Street by Jewish real estate agents from the market square, who sent to them a Jewish apartment house whose owners were Poles.

The Lipińskis had bought this property inhabited by Jewish tenants in 1928 from the Jew Werner, and things stayed that way. The new owners also preferred to rent to Jews, with whom -- in contrast to Poles -- they had no problems. The Jews paid on time, sometimes even in advance, they did not drink, did not raise a rumpus, always somehow came to terms with the owners. Besides this, nearly all of the residents of Zamkowa 8, which was in the center of town close to the market square, were Jews.

On the ground floor there was even a Jewish kosher pub, which had been established by the Werners; it filled the entire courtyard with the odor of goose meat, fish, fried onion - Jan Lipiński remembers this odor to this day.

Zamkowa 8 was perhaps the symbol of a Jewish apartment house. Werner had built it for himself and his family; from his former apartment one entered the "bower"-resting on beautiful, sculpted columns of a glass-enclosed veranda with a

double roof. The outside, tin one could be moved aside, leaving a second one --plaited from reeds. In this "bower" the Werners celebrated the Feast of Tabernacles; the other tenants put up tents in the courtyard. The "bower" attested to the affluence of a Jewish home; it adorned only one other Sandomierz apartment house, right by the synagogue.

Just at that time the Lipińskis did not have a vacant apartment, but they didn't want to pass up the chance to earn some money, so they sublet one of their three rooms to the Lewinkopfs, who looked reliable and cultured and paid well -- in advance, in dollars. So the owners gave them the largest room, furnished, with a view of the Vistula embankment, ravines. They also permitted their tenants to use the kitchen, where they ate, washed in a basin - water had to be carried in all the way from the market square, and the toilet was in the courtyard.

The war had just started - so Mrs. Lipiński registered the Lewinkopfs like all of her other tenants; she kept a registration book which she had in her possession for many years after the occupation, but it was lost after the move from Zamkowa Street.

The Lewinkopfs resided in Sandomierz quite legally. Their names and signatures (the father signed for the under age little Jerzy) appear on many documents drawn up by the Jewish community for the German authorities. Today these documents are stored in the Sandomierz State Archives. Among these documents are registration cards for temporary residence, stating when and to whose residence they had moved in, from whose residence they had moved out, who registered them, etc. The surname "Kosiński" also appears on many "censuses of the Jewish population," if only on the "list of Jews who had come to Sandomierz," "who had taken up residence in Sandomierz in 1940, 1941, and 1942."

According to these documents, Moses Lewinkopf,* son of Nusyn and Basia, merchant from Łódź (Gdansk Street 74), was born on 18 October 1891 in Zamość.

Elżbieta Lewinkopf (housewife) - daughter of Meier and Sura - was born on 6 January 1899 inŁódź.

As for Jerzy Nikodem - 14 June 1933, also in Łódź.

To say the truth, they didn't fit in at Zamkowa Street at all. Though they were Jews, like all the other residents, they were clearly "better," assimilated. They spoke only in Polish, they didn't celebrate the Sabbath; and from the first glance they stood out from the rest of the Jews, who spoke only Yiddish and broken Polish, wore gabardines, skullcaps, had side curls, and on holidays wore talliths. There were a few rather affluent families, the Rajnbergers, for example, but most of the others were petty merchants, like the Bermans, owners of a fruit and fish stand. In the basement, on the other hand, lived the real Jewish poor, among others the porter Little Nusen with his twelve children.

But even the more affluent Jews lived modestly; they "let out" their apartments and moved in with Mrs. Lipiński, because it was cheaper. They slept on the most ordinary iron beds, their children attended Jewish school for only a

---

* Before the war he was also a professor at the Grammar School of the Merchants' Association in Łódź.

3

few years, after which they helped their parents in business, learned how to trade, during the occupation mainly in cigarettes.

The Lewinkopfs, in contrast, apparently not only had money but also connections; since for the almost a year and a half they lived at Zamkowa Street they never worked, despite the strict order to work that had been imposed on Jews from almost the start of the occupation. Others were driven in hundreds to the local glass factory and to public works projects.

They, on the other hand, rose rather late to breakfasts served by Mrs. Lipiński; they read newspapers, and waited for mail from Łódź. And after that -- looking elegant, stylish, he shaved, she always perfumed, they took young Jerzy by the hand and went out. They returned toward evening, speaking with little Jerzy as with an adult.

His chums called Jan Lipiński the "Jewish uncle." And indeed -- as he said -- he "argued in Jewish"; he had been brought up among Jews, spent his childhood and early youth among them. He liked them a lot -- they were fair, reliable, "money-wise," which made a big impression on him. Though his brother Tadeusz had graduated from college, Jan would have none of that; he preferred to trade with his pals from the back-yard in whatever came to hand -- cigarettes, fine-tooth combs for lice, rabbit skins from the countryside.

So he was always in the know about what was going on in the back-yard, and he remembers clearly how glad the youngsters were that another boy had arrived -- Jurek Lewinkopf. They often tried to get him to play various games, started conversations with him, but he always resolutely, patronizingly refused and dismissed them with contempt. He said that he didn't play with Jews, for he was a Pole -- Jurek Kosiński!

They laughed, of course, and didn't believe him. After all, his name was Lewinkopf, he lived at Zamkowa Street, and, besides, all one had to do was look at him, not to speak of his mother! Despite this, he kept saying that he was a Pole -- Kosiński! To prove this, he used to show a medallion around his neck and recited entire prayers in correct Polish. Not only *Our Father* but also *Hail Mary* and *I Believe in* God!

He completely squelched them with this; they glared at him with fury and admiration. Most of them spoke Polish poorly -- ungrammatically, with an accent.

And with the exception of young Jan Lipiński, the only Pole among the back-yard clan, none of them could recite a prayer, for where would they have learned one?

One time they accosted him outside, tried to entice him to play a game, when he was walking with his mother, who didn't pull him away from them, didn't *forbid* anything, but only said softly: "Jerzy, remember about the accent!" She reminded him that if he played with these lads, he might pick up their accent. She didn't have to persuade him very strongly - he had no intention of joining them.

In the fall and winter, the back-yard activities moved inside to the corridor, which Mrs. Lipiński cleaned and polished every day, like the entire apartment house. The corridor was filled with kids of all ages, who ran wild, slid down the banisters. They were all there, with the exception of Jurek Lewinkopf, who didn't even peek outside, even though he could hear their squeals through the door. One must admit, he sure had grit -- he was only a child, he must have wanted to get in on the fun, but he never joined his peers, he never left his parents' side.

To get under his skin, to get his goat, the other kids nicknamed him "Josek." "Josek, come here!" -- they called, which obviously infuriated him even more,

gave him fits. He kept repeating that his name was Jurek, Jurek Kosiński, but they didn't believe him. At Zamkowa 8 there were no Jews with Polish first names. There were Abram, Lejzor, Chaim, Fajwele, but Jurek? They thought that maybe he had "converted," "transcribed," as it was called, which sometimes happened among Jews, especially wealthy and educated ones. So the gang despised the supposed convert and sissy, nicknamed him Josek, but they were also a little jealous of him -- after all, he was somebody better.

He didn't even try to stand up to one of them, but he did badger the younger kids. A few times he gave a thrashing to little Berman for calling him "Josek" and also his contemporary and closest neighbor --   Rebecca Blusztajn. And when -- despite this -- she tried to drag him out into the corridor, he kicked her, spat on her, called her a dirty Jewess, so that she finally left him alone.

The Lipińskis -- as their children remember -- talked between themselves about his behavior. They thought that he had "gone bad" -- after all, his parents were so cultured, likeable! They blamed this on their age: Kosińska already had strands of gray hair, Kosiński - a bald spot, pot-belly. For those times they were too old to have such a young son.

Living together with them presented no problems, however. They were extremely polite, charming, especially the husband - calm, good natured. He was very much interested in politics, and in the evenings always asked Mr. Lipiński, who ran a carpenter's shop, what was new in town, what the people were saying. Kosiński was very obliging. Once, when Lipinska couldn't get soap, he offered to make it himself from fat, saying he knew all about this, because before the war he had owned a chemicals factory. But Lipinska managed to get the soap; the shortages were just beginning.

The oldest of the Lipiński daughters, Zofia Rogowska, who was already married at that time, lived in nearby Miedzygorze, where her husband was the steward of a landed estate. Sometimes she used to come with him to Sandomierz to visit her parents, and she even met the Lewinkopfs, who later asked their hosts if it wouldn't be possible to move in with their daughter. Hard times were ·coming for Jews, and they would like to move to the country, far away from people, for Zamkowa Street was right in the center of town, they were too visible there. They would pay well and in advance and wouldn't cause any trouble.

"But son-in-law Rogowski" -- Tadeusz Lipiński recalls -"didn't know them well enough. He couldn't make up his mind, he wasn't the owner, just the steward, and he was afraid of losing his job, the more so as he had small children. Besides, this wasn't an out-of-the-way place; on the contrary, there were a lot of people -- workers, residents."

People simply thought the Lewinkopfs were looking for another, quieter address; they couldn't stay under the Lipińskis' roof forever. Could anyone have imagined that they were perhaps thinking of escape, a hideout? The occupation had just begun, and no one -- least of all the residents of Zamkowa 8 -- had any inkling of the impending Holocaust; they were unaware of what was afoot. And some of them even said to the Poles with satisfaction -- your times have passed!

Mr. Tadeusz Lipiński remembers that once he was picked up for violating the curfew and that the translators at Gestapo headquarters were Jews -- members of the *Judenrat.*

So the residents of Zamkowa Street went about their business as if nothing had happened. Just a few months before the Nazis established a ghetto, the sly real estate agents from the market square, "factors," as they were called, even wanted to buy the apartment house from the Lipińskis, offered a lot of money; but the latter turned them down flat, even though they would soon be forced to leave their home and live with strangers. At Zamkowa Street and neighboring streets -- Żydowska and Joselewicza -- a ghetto was created.

* * *

Toward the end of March 1941, the Lewinkopfs packed their bags and politely took leave of their hosts. They didn't say where they were going or to whom, and thełżs didn't ask them, for the persecutions had already started. Stars of David, orders, prohibitions, roundups to concentration camps, soon also a ghetto -- created in the spring of 1942, closed in the summer, evacuated toward the end of October.

All of the residents of Zamkowa 8 found themselves in the ghetto, and they perished along with the other Sandomierz Jews in the gas ovens of Bełżec. Perhaps one of the twelve children of the porter Nusen -- a communist who before the war had gone to the Soviet Union - survived, but no one knows this. Little Nusen was lucky -- just "before the ghetto" he was run over on the street by a car. People said that God took mercy on him and did not let him watch the death of his eleven brothers and sisters.

* * *

Not until 1968 did the Lipińskis learn from a Słowo Ludu journalist[*], who somehow managed to find them, that the Lewinkopfs had also survived and that the "little one" supposedly had written some "anti-Polish" book! Mrs. Maria Lipiński even gave an interview about him, her recollections of him are not positive.

" ... "He was then seven or eight years old" -- she said. "He was small and the Lewinkopfs had a lot of trouble with him. He was mean. He hated Jews the most

---

[*] T. Wiacek, *"Słowo Ludu,"*No. 1/61, 9 May 1968.

of all. I remember how he used to plague old Blusztajn. He couldn't stomach little Rebecca Blusztajn, who was about his age. He treated Poles with respect, but he couldn't stand Jews."

Her children later held this against her, for, though she had told the truth, it wasn't the whole truth. And the journalist wasn't really interested in that.

"Why" - Tadeusz Lipiński says – "you can't possibly leave out the fact that they survived thanks to escaping from their Jewishness, cutting themselves off from it completely. In my opinion, Moses Lewinkopf -- I only understand this today -- already then probably had a presentiment of the Holocaust."

Though it was only the beginning of the occupation and most of his compatriots were living as if nothing had happened, he was the only one who seemed to understand something. If only that Zamkowa 8 was not a safe place for his family. Already then he had tried to move to Międzygórze, to the provinces. To change his surname to a Polish one -- little Jurek even then kept saying that his name was Kosiński!

Moses also probably made his son aware that being a Jew carried a mortal danger. And it would be interesting to know what he said, since the seven-year-old took this so much to heart. He became so frightened that he gave his little compatriots a wide berth. He beat them and kicked them. He wanted to be only Jurek Kosiński and not Josek Lewinkopf.

CHAPTER 2

Gołębicka 3

From the registration documents in the Sandomierz Archives we learn that on 31 March 1941 the Lewinkopfs "came for a temporary stay" to the late Wacław Skobel -- wagoner, room painter. To his new imposing wooden house with a porch. The house still stands, but it is quite run down. To Gołębicka 3, now renamed Zeromski Street, inhabited almost entirely by Poles. They rented half of the house that Skobel had set aside for tenants, leaving the other half for himself and his family.

The Justyński siblings remember them from this period. Maria Medrzak (1932) and Henryk Justyński (1934) still live in Sandomierz, while Bogumita Staron (1931) now lives in Łódź.

They distinctly remember little Jerzy Lewinkopf, who almost every day used to come with his parents to the Lewinkopfs' colleague and neighbor -- Stefek Salamonowicz. The Salamonowiczs, like the Lewinkopfs, were Łódź Jews; they probably knew each other from way back, in any case they appeared to be well acquainted. They also, right after the outbreak of the war, found themselves in Sandomierz, Mrs. Salamonowicz1s home town. Her parents, the old Spiros, who owned almost half of Opatowska Street, were among the richest Sandomierz Jews. At least five apartment houses and a mercer's shop. They had a servant, a nanny for Stefan who kept close on his heels.

As Jews were wont to do, they lived at the market square, of course, in their apartment house at Opatowska 4. The Justyńskis, on the other hand, lived in the adjacent house as one of the few Polish families there. And on the Sabbath, they made pocket money by lighting fires for neighbors, lighting candles in candlesticks.

So they were brought up entirely among Jews; their parents completely accepted this -- it doesn't matter if someone is a Jew, they always. repeated.

The Spiros, as well as the Salamonowiczs, belonged to the Sandomierz upper crust, for they were not only affluent but also cultured, assimilated. Probably only Hanka Spiro-Salamonowicz's granny, who was still living at that time, was an Orthodox Jewess in a wig, speaking Yiddish. But Hanka's father, old Spiro, spoke only Polish and was a man of the world, a dapper Dan. She herself looked like an "artist." Beautiful, chic, intelligent, with a secondary school leaving certificate. Her husband, Jerzy Salamonowicz, was a rich factory owner, a chemical engineer by education.

Just about everyone who counted for anything visited the Spiros and Salamonowiczs, including the Lewinkopfs, who were also very cultured and affluent. The Lewinkopfs had two maids, who came to their house at Gołębicka every day. One did the cleaning, the other the cooking. The latter, Juliana Bajacz, still lives in Sandomierz, but she lives alone and is *afraid* of letting in strangers, so I wasn't able to talk with her. She was referred to the Lewinkopfs by the Justyńskis; she was their grandmother's foster-child, an orphan from an orphanage. Mrs. Justyński recommended her to the Lewinkopfs, who -- through the Spiros -- were urgently looking for someone, because Mrs. Lewinkopf was all thumbs, she always had had a maid. Juliana Bajacz was treated well by Mrs. Lewinkopf, who didn't interfere, was generous, gave away old things, made her a gift of a golden ring.

The Lewinkopfs lived with the Skobels only through the fall and winter. Approximately from May to September they moved to the summer resort in Rokitek, which today is a district of Sandomierz but at that time was outside of town. One could get there by foot - from Ucho lgielny down the steps and from there through the valley and fields. Mrs. Zofia Staroń used to go there often and even today remembers this wonderful place.

The cottage was quite ordinary, probably even with a straw roof, but it was beautifully situated. In a large garden full of fruit trees, bushes and flowers. In a hollow with a beautiful view of the Vistula, hills, ravines and the valley.

No neighbors anywhere, complete isolation. Just the owner of the house, Marianna Pasiowa, the Justyńskis' aunt, who for the summer moved into the kitchen, leasing the rest of the house to the Lewinkopfs. From time to time her son used to drop in from Podwale. On visits to his mother he baked bread "on the sly"; he worked in a bakery shop, where he always managed to gather up some flour, so at the cottage there was never a shortage of fresh, hot bread, for which people in Sandomierz had to stand in lines for hours.

* * *

The Justyński kids, on the other hand, represented an entirely different world. There were five of them, their mother worked in a dairy, the father made shoes - - at home, because he couldn't afford to rent a workshop. In the cellar he raised pigs, illegally, of course, under the punishment of death if he got caught. He also rented gardens, the children had to help him gather in the crops, arrange the fruits in the cellar and then sell them. Despite their poverty, the children were clean, well-cared for, attended school, but how could they compare with the Lewinkopfs and Salamonowiczs?

None the less, both sets of parents looked favorably on their children's friendship with each other. They were always inviting the Justyński youngsters over, asking if they would come tomorrow. The Lewinkopfs and Salamonowiczs were clearly pleased that their sons were playing with Poles and not with Jews, of whom there were many, including the richest ones, at the market square.

So they played with each other almost every day, most often at Stefan's house, but sometimes at the Justyńskis', where they ate -- from the same bowl--foods that were exotic to Stetan as well as to Jurek. There was potato soup and soups with dumplings, scrambled eggs with flour. They ate it up with relish though Stefan and Jurek were constantly urged to eat even more by the servants. They were given foreign delicacies, even though it was wartime and the country was occupied, and poverty was all around.

Of course, it was often obvious that they came from two different worlds. Henryk Justyński remembers an incident when the boys pretended that they were draft horses and he with his younger brother Adam were the drivers. They had sticks that were the buggy whips! Old Mr. Spiro saw this as he came out into the yard and loudly commented why it was that his grandson and Jurek Lewinkopf are the horses while the Justyński kids are the drivers. It should have been otherwise! He said it with such force that instantly the roles were reversed.

Little Henryk Justyński was naturally offended but how he could discuss such matters with old Mr. Spiro?

Mrs. Zofia Staroń remembers how Mrs. Lewinkopf gave them to understand that she had higher status and whose place was where. It happened that on occasion her voice would take on an unpleasant tone and she would give orders -- don't go there, don't touch that! Mrs. Salamonowicz was much more pleasant and gracious. She, however, was a neighbor and also Zofia's mother's schoolmate (they both finished grammar school together). She would address Mrs. Justyński by her first name, but the other would reply using more formal language. After all, she was speaking to the daughter of old Mr. Spiro who was also the wife of engineer Salamonowicz. Even though he would come from Sandomierz only to visit his in-laws, he was held in very high regard. During the occupation he probably had a position on the Sandomierz Judenrat.

The kids played with young Lewinkopf only because he was Stefan's friend. To tell the truth, they did not like him much -- he was different from the other children. He seemed more mature, more serous, sidelines, more a spectator than a participant. He shunned lively games like races, scraps, horseplay. He hated digging in the sand or doing anything that could get him dirty -- right away he shook himself off; to this day they remember that gesture which seemed so funny to them. He was very clean, with his clothes perfectly pressed, beautifully dressed -- hand knitted sweaters, short pants, stylish low shoes, while during the same time more and more Jewish children were wearing rags and going around bare-footed. What is most important, however, he was very intelligent, but malicious, domineering, swaggering, always getting his way.

Once they were playing in a garden rented by Mr. Justyński, and Jurek and Stefan -- mostprobably out of stupidity or lack of imagination - had put little Marysia into a baby carriage and with all of their might had pushed it down the hill. The carriage raced down the hill like an arrow, but fortunately was stopped by a tree and the child was not injured, though it could have ended in tragedy. The little girl only shed some tears, was frightened out of her wits. Stefan clearly was sorry for what they had done. Jurek, on the other hand, just laughed - he could do anything! His doting parents, especially his mother, never punished him, never chided him.

When they went out in the evenings to the Salamonowiczs to play cards, they didn't want him to be left alone, that is, only with their hosts - in Sandomierz with the Skobels, in Rokitnik with Pasiowa. So they asked Zosia Justyńska to keep him company; though she was only two years older than him, she was serious, sensible, and willingly agreed - they always left sweets, fruits. Already before the war, Zosia had finished first grade, she could read and write, and since she liked to play school she also tried to play with Jurek, but this didn't work out. Though he was younger than she, he also already knew how to read and write, maybe even better than she could?

Besides, he knew everything, had been everywhere. So when she pointed something out to him, corrected him, tried to teach him, he became infuriated and carried on like a spoiled brat! It was the same when they played "fish" -- he always had to win, he hated to lose, even at cards!

They mostly remember the games. After all, they were only children and didn't pay attention to what was going on around them. And though, for example, Jews had already been forbidden to enter the park, they ignored this completely. Many times, when no one was watching them, they used to take Stefan and Jurek by the hand and run quickly out of the gate, chasing each other and shouting! And despite the fact that Jurek had a very Semitic appearance, the gendarmes paid no attention to them; in the provinces the terror unquestionably was less severe.

The more so as neither Jurek nor Stefan, nor their parents for that matter, wore the Star of David. As regards the Lewinkopfs, this is understandable; they were strangers, few people knew them. But the Salamonowiczs? Especially Mrs. Salamonowicz, from one of the most prominent local Jewish families? In any case, they didn't wear the Star of David, which was even commented on by the parents of the Justyński kids.

The children continued to play with each other as if nothing was wrong, when, at the beginning of 1942, the Germans started to create a ghetto in the center of Sandomierz -- including the region of Zydowska, Zamkowa, Joselewicza Streets -- and to herd in Jews from the vicinity - from Ćmielow, Połańca, Klimonotowa,

Ozarowa. The ghetto was open for quite a long time; it was probably closed toward the end of August and liquidated near the end of October, as one of the last - almost to the very end the Sandomierz *Judenrat* continuedto buy off the Germans, postponing the sentence.

In the opinion of the Justyński siblings, the Lewinkopfs did not go to the ghetto. Today it is hard to determine this; be that as it *may,* long before the ghetto was closed, they simply disappeared. The Justyńskis lost touch with them.

Neither can one find the Lewinkopfs on lists of Jews of the Sandomierz ghetto stored in the Sandomierz Archives (but these lists are incomplete).

Little Stefan Salamonowicz and his nanny, the Pole Zofia Kaczorowska, also disappeared. I later discovered that, pretending to be his mother, she lived through the occupation with him in Otwock near Warsaw. Old Spiro also disappeared; he also hid himself and survived in Warsaw.

Jerzy Salamonowicz was arrested -- apparently in a street roundup -- just "before the ghetto"; he was taken to a concentration camp, but he survived. Hanka Spiro-Salamonowicz hid herself, but she got caught; she was locked up in a cell at the market square. The Justyński kids used to bring her food and water, which the watchman Stec, their parents' acquaintance, passed on to her when no one was looking. On the way to the concentration camp, she managed to jump the train and get to Warsaw, where she rented an apartment, and on Sundays she used to come to Otwock to visit little Stefan, who called her "auntie."

They were lucky, and people - as people are wont to do - said that "money was responsible," because the entire family survived. Apart from them, literally only a few Sandomierz Jews survived. Nusek Fiszman and his wife, who were also very rich. Chilek Las, who joined the partisans, and Róża Mała, who today bears the name Rosa Mala and lives in the United States; she had been concealed by her fiance, a Pole named Bażant, who still lives in Sandomierz. He didn't marry her, however, for -- as he says -- she had "her faith" and he had his, and this did not presage a good marriage. For how could two faiths sleep on one pillow?

CHAPTER 3

Za Bramką 4

According to the registration files in the Sandomierz Archives, on 16 August 1942 the Lewinkopfs registered at Za Bramką 4 Street. The registration book is signed -- not very legibly -- by S. Morgen(?).

Za Bramkq 4, which today is only a by-street, still exists; it runs parallel to Zamkowa Street, from where one has to go -- as is usual in Sandomierz -- down steps to the ravines. Only one wooden cottage without a number stands here today. Its two residents -- old women - didn't want to let me in. Besides, they wouldn't have said anything anyway. One of them is bed-ridden, the other walks with difficulty and is hard of hearing. They couldn't understand what I wanted. Who was I looking for?

In the opinion the people I talked with in Sandomierz, the Lewinkopfs most probably never resided at Za Bramką 4. In any case, they do not associate them with this address at all. To the end of their stay in Sandomierz they lived with the Skobels, and from there they disappeared.

Another strange thing is the late date of the registration entry - 16 August 1942, two weeks before the closing of the ghetto. Could they still have registered themselves outside the ghetto at this late date? In the Sandomierz Archives I was told that this was impossible; they only could have registered on one of the streets within the ghetto, but Za Bramką 4, which was far away from the center of town, was not within the ghetto.

What is more, the registration card - unlike those from Zamkowa and Gołębicka - is filled out very sloppily, hastily, with mistakes and deletions. Most importantly, what is missing is a notation of departure from the Skobels, though there is such anotation of departure from the Lipińskis. The seal with the registration date is completely illegible, like the signature of "head of the department for movement of the population."

In the column "staying with whom," instead of the exact surname, first name and address of the new host, there is the entry "in their own apartment," which was certainly not true. Though on previous cards there was the exact Łódź address, on this card, in the column "place of permanent residence," there is the entry "Sandomierz - Za Bramką" but it was deleted, corrected, changed to Łódź, but with no street. In previous places of registration, each member of the family had a separate registration card, but here - only Moses Lewinkopf.

Mr. Henryk Justyński thinks that they registered themselves there "only on paper" and to "throw off the scent." They had been planning their escape, so they wanted to put the authorities on the wrong trail. They had long since left Sandomierz, but officially they were living at Za Bramką. Maybe in this way they "took the heat off" Skobel, because they had taken flight from his home and he might still have to answer for that!

But, perhaps by some miracle, they somehow registered themselves, tried to live, but in the end had to go to the ghetto. So did they decide to run away then?

For they chose an ideal place -- far away from the center, in a ravine, among meadows, fields and cows, with cottages distant from each other. To find a house number there is no easy task, so it was all the harder to guess whether this was still Za Bramką or already nearby Podwale.

CHAPTER 4

Sacks of Flour

Mrs. Maria Czechow (1901) and her younger sister, Zofia Iżykowska, who now lives in Łódź but spent the occupation in her native Sandomierz, also remember them. Zofia helped her sister and brother-in-law Aleksy Czechow run a bakery shop at the market square, where just about everybody dropped in, not just for bread but also for gossip, information.

Moses Lewinkopf also used to come here. They established a rather close relationship with him, for -- like the Iżykowskis - he was from Łódź, and compatriots always seem to find a common language. Aleksy Czech liked to talk with him about politics, which interested both of them. Aleksy rather liked Jews, with whom he worked -- for nearly all of the shops at the market square were owned by Jews. Mrs. Izykowski's husband Roman, however, was deeply involved in the underground Home Army and had no contacts with Lewinkopf, except for one occasion; he asked Lewinkopf, who was educated and knew foreign languages, for help in buying a typewriter. Lewinkopf promised to help, but in the end Roman's fellow conspirators somehow managed to get one on their own.

The bakers always set aside fresh bread for Lewinkopf; bread was always in short supply, because they could bake only a limited amount. At other times they took bread home, to Długosz Street, where Lewinkopf sometimes used to drop by. He lived not far from there, with Skobel, who delivered flour to the bakery.

Lewinkopf always came alone; only once did he bring his wife and son. That's hardly surprising, for they were the personification of Jewish looks, though Mrs. Lewinkopf somehow tried to hide this. On this occasion she wore a large peasant shawl on her head that hardly matched her city clothes and appearance and made her large, aquiline nose even more prominent.

Moses Lewinkopf, however, could pass for a Pole, and so people pitied him. He had a chance to survive were it not for his wife and son or -- as they put it in the bakery -- two sacks of flour that he had to carry on his back.

* * *

Somehow, he managed to carry this burden, for the entire trio suddenly disappeared. No one heard that they had gone to the ghetto; no one saw them there. And to the very end the ghetto was half open, and many Jews used to slip out to the bakery for bread, but Lewinkopf was not among them, and he certainly would have come to the bakery had he been in the ghetto.

Of course, people asked Skobel, "What has happened to your tenants?" He answered that he knew nothing. They just suddenly vanished, like a stone in water!

And it was only toward the end of the war, when he was no longer in any danger, that he told people that he had transported them out of Sandomierz, loaded them onto his cart and taken them to Radomyśl on the river San. To a Catholic priest who was supposed to find a hiding place for them. He delivered them safely, thank God, but he had no idea whether they survived.

People did not dare ask why he had done this. Did he simply want to help them? Or was it for money? For he took a terrible risk! He was a simple, decent, worthy man. Resourceful and hard-working; he cared about his family and new home and seized every opportunity to make money.

* * *

It wasn't until after the war that he learned that the Lewinkopfs had survived. He was told this by Aleksy Czech, whose son-in-law, Roman łżykowski, met them in Łódź in 1945. Much later, of course, he also learned from Czech that little Jerzy Lewinkopf had become a writer and supposedly had "described" the Poles!

"That little beautiful boy who played in my garden?" - Skobel asked in surprise. – "Whom I took to the country? Whom I saved from the ghetto? Can that be possible?"

* * *

Wacław Skobel is no longer alive; his wife, who still lives in their house at Żeromskiego 33, recently suffered a stroke and is in very poor health. Skobel junior was born after the war and knows nothing about the Lewinkopfs, except that they once lived in his house.

The father often mentioned them, but the boy paid little attention, for he was more interested in playing ball outside.

He only remembers that his father most often talked of how he had saved the Lewinkopfs from the ghetto, how he had taken them out of Sandomierz in his cart. On the way, the father used to tell, they seemed to be petrified with fear; they hardly moved during the entire journey, did not utter a single word. But he was more afraid than they were, especially when crossing the bridge over the Vistula; he was sure that -- if they got caught, they would be drowned immediately!

During the entire journey he prayed for all he was worth; he didn't spare the whip and drove on the horse -- faster, faster! But Providence apparently guided him and watched over him, for he delivered them there safely!

* * *

However, it wasn't until the fifties that the Justyńskis found out that the Lewinkopfs had survived. Adam Justyński was attending the university in Łódź and sometimes used to visit the Salamonowiczs, who had returned to their native city and had renewed their friendship with the Lewinkopfs, who now bore the name Kosiński.

It was at the Salamonowiczs that he met young Jerzy Kosiński, but only once. And once was enough for him, since the lad had changed very little. During a game of cards Jerzy soon caused a row -- he always wanted to win, to decide, to dominate. To be -- as before -- only the coachman. Adam Justyński, however, no longer had to put up with such behavior.

That is why he had no desire to see Kosiński, years later, when the latter came to Poland as a famous person; and despite the fact that Adam's brothers and sisters urged him to do so, since they planned to go to Warsaw -- for them the famous writer was still little Jerzy Lewinkopf, their childhood chum. They had read *The Painted Bird,* of course, but they thought that it was based on later, apparently tragic, experiences.

After all, in Sandomierz he had enjoyed a pretty good life. Despite the impending catastrophe, he still was -- at least for them -- the elegant little lord, waited on, fed by a nanny, spending the summer in a vacation resort. A pampered only child living in plenty, whose wise, loving parents had saved him in the nick of time from the ghetto, the fate of his compatriots.

The Justyńskis were disappointed, surprised, that in his frequent interviews he spoke of Kazimierz on the Vistula, Cracow, the Tatras but never of Sandomierz, where - and that was the most important -- he safely lived through nearly two and a half years of the occupation.

He never visited Sandomierz, even though Jews from all over the world come here. They visit the Jewish school, the synagogue, the former home of the Jewish commune. They take pictures, look for traces, shed tears, express their sorrow over the destruction, the decay of the city.

He, on the contrary, though he spoke often of memory, of his Jewish roots, the emotion that always comes over him in Poland -- never uttered a word or made a single gesture. Nothing, absolutely nothing.

CHAPTER 5

The Little Black Spider

Toward the end of August 1939, Mr. Andrzej Migdałek, today a retired engineer from Bielsko-Biała, and his sister Ewa Dziadek, a dentist from Żory, fled with their parents from Silesia just before the Germans entered. Fate brought the family to Dąbrowa Rzeczycka near Rozwadów, now Tarnobrzeg province, where the father, a teacher, found a job in the local four-grade elementary school and -- an apartment.

The quarters were located in a wooden residential barrack that belonged to the commune and was situated some distance from the village. The neighboring barrack, an identical one, belonged to one of the peasants, Andrzej Warchoł, who occupied one of the apartments and rented out the others. At that time one of the apartments was empty. It had been vacated by the Liebeskinds, who, like the rest of the Jews from the vicinity, in the summer of 1942 had gone to the assembly point in Zaklików, where they were killed on the spot - they had refused to board the trains for Treblinka.

And it was probably in September, at the latest in October, that Warchoł brought *new* tenants to the apartment -- the Kosińskis, as he introduced them.

"Jesus, Mary, and Joseph, some have left, others have come!" - Mrs. Migdałek moaned, fearing for her two children - seven-year-old Andrzej called Bumek (1934) and nine-year-old Ewa (1932). All one had to do was look at the Kosińskis and it was clear that they were Jews!

Especially Mrs. Kosiński, the most Semitic-looking one -- raven-haired, black-eyed, with a prominent aquiline nose, and little Jurek, her miniature - slender, swarthy, long-legged. "The Little Black Spider," as they called him. "Old man" Kosiński could get lost in a crowd, he wasn't conspicuous, but even he had the appearance of a Jewish intellectual -- stooping, balding, in round steel-framed glasses that attracted attention -- who in the village wore glasses?

Besides them, there were three-year--old Henio, a plump, fair blond but with Semitic features, and his nanny Katarzyna, an oldish, gray-haired Polish woman, who supposedly had saved him at the last moment. The tot called the Kosiriskis "auntie" and "uncle," while they made no secret of the fact that this was the child of friends who had gone to Oswięcim or Treblinka.

At least this is what Mrs. Kosiński told Mrs. Migdałek, for they quickly struck up neighborly relations. The two barracks were separated only by a fence with a gate that was always open, and the two women saw each other every day. Mrs. Migdałek even invited the Kosińskis to the first Christmas Eve supper here to show the village that she was not afraid of the new neighbors and to emphasize that village intellectuals should become friends, stick together.

Mr. Andrzej Migdałek remembers how they broke bread together instead of a holy wafer and that the only dish was sour soup with potatoes - they were as poor as Job - and it was there that he learned was hunger is. The land around Dąbrowa was very barren, sandy, little could grow there; so the people ate pigweed soup, beetroot soup, sour soup, potatoes, rationed bread made from chaff and sweepings, marmalade made from beets.

However, the village received the Kosińskis very well, especially Mr. Kosiński, whom they titled "professor," and Mrs. Kosiński – "the professor's wife." Most of the older residents of the village were illiterate, so they respected Mr. Kosiński, who really was very intelligent, educated, well-informed about politics, fluent in several languages.

All of the people, of course, knew or suspected that the Kosińskis were Jews, but it never entered anyone's mind to inform the Germans, who were stationed in nearby Zaklików or Radomyśl. The village was really a god-forsaken hole, poor but religious, decent, understanding that "these are also people and also want to live."

To be sure, every time he passed by Warchoł's barrack stupid Jaś Chołody would shout: *"Jude, raus!"*, and the local kids called out "Jews, little Jews!" after Jurek and Henio, but so what? On such occasions Mrs. Warchoł would immediately rush out with a broom, yell at them to shut up, for otherwise the Germans would bum everyone alive, the entire village!

Meanwhile, the Kosińskis lay low; they tried to be as inconspicuous as possible. Only the professor ventured outside the Warchoł enclosure; and, to say the truth, he almost seemed to slink away. His collar was always raised, his face covered, head down, eyes fixed on the ground. He never greeted anyone, passed without a word, though people also said that he had poor eyesight (he did wear thick lenses). He most often slunk away to neighboring Kępa, which had more fertile land and where one could buy something to eat - potatoes, vegetables, milk, and butter. In Dąbrowa almost no one kept a cow; there were a lot of goats and rabbits, which ate anything. And only millet, rye, buckwheat, beets, and potatoes grew here.

Soon, however, the professor stopped slinking and began to go to Kępa in a free and easy manner; he saw how he had been received and felt safer. In any case, in the spring of 1943 he took up work in the local state purchasing center as a recording clerk and also started to give lessons in secondary school subjects, for which he was paid in kind - milk, butter, potatoes.

"The Little Black Spider," the professor's wife, and Henio with his nanny almost never left the confines of the Warchoł property; and when they did, they only went across the fence, to the Migdałeks'. In the beginning, Mrs. Kosiński, who had the "worst" appearance, rarely even went into the yard, except to go to the outdoor toilet, and at those times Mrs. Migdałek used to admire her beautiful low-cut dresses. Mrs. Kosiński also almost never showed up in church, but Jurek and his father went every Sunday. They never stood at the altar, however, but in the comer, on the side, and always returned quickly.

They stayed in Dąbrowa until the end of April 1945, so "the Little Black Spider'" spent two and a half years in their apartment in the barrack and in the yard. More precisely -- on the fence and "hollered," as the Migdałek kids said, or constantly whined:

"Ewka, Bumek! Come out and play! Or can I come over to your house?"

He could only go to their house, nowhere else, so he was forced to keep company with them; no other children lived in the barracks. So they played with each other almost every day, most often at the Migdałeks' -- their yard belonged to the commune, so it was really nobody's, but Jurek's yard belonged to Warchoł, who often chopped wood there and didn't want kids getting under foot.

The Migdałek children also liked to go over to Jurek's house, for he lived in more comfortable surroundings than they. Their teacher's apartment had only beds of boards covered with straw and bed-spreads. At the Kosińskis', however, there was decent furniture that had belonged to the Liebeskinds. In the parlor -- a couch, wardrobe, two twin-beds on which the Kosińskis slept with Jurek. In the kitchen -- a table, chairs, cupboard, and a bed of boards for the nanny and Henio.

The wooden barracks, which were plastered, were called "sawmill bunkhouses"; they had been built during the time of Duke Lubomirski for workers of the sawmill, which was later run by the Liebeskinds. These structures were also called "farm hands' living quarters," though the apartments in them were quite decent, better by far than the crowded, primitive peasants' cottages. A large, high- ceilinged parlor, a kitchen with a pantry, and a cellar, to which one descended by a ladder. The porch was entwined with greenery. In the yard were a well and a row of latrines -- a separate one for each family -- and boxes for fuel and rabbits.

Jurek hardly every played with Henio, for he didn't like him very much. As an only child, Jurek was not used to the presence of another boy, the more so as Henio was only a few years' old and constantly bothered him -- always taking something, crying. On account of his experiences, separation from his parents, Henio was a rather difficult child, "ornery," as Mrs. Kosiński complained. "You can tear his head off, but he'll still do as he pleases!" -- she said.

She didn't bother about him at all. As Katarzyna put it, Mrs. Kosiński had two left hands as far as he was concerned and a rather cold attitude toward him; she never cuddled him, never kissed him, and it was apparent that he was not her son. On the other hand, Katarzyna, his guardian angel, adored him. She never let him out of her sight and didn't like Mrs. Kosiński for her coldness to "little Henio."

✳ ✳ ✳

Father Eugeniusz Okoń of Radomyśl on the river San, a well-known figure of the twenty-year interwar period, had brought the Kosińskis to Dąbrowa. He was not only a priest but also a leftist peasant activist, leader of the Radical Peasants' Party, who had served two terms in the Diet as a deputy of the Polish Peasants'

Party of the Left. He had lived several years in Warsaw, where he had many connections and acquaintances.

He also loved cards, good alcohol, and women; in Warsaw he had a concubine and two daughters whom he raised, supported. And officially for this reason, but unofficially for "stirring up the peasants," "for revolutionizing the countryside," the episcopate in Przemyśl suspended him in his priestly functions. He was later forced to "repent in sackcloth and ashes" and retire to do penance in a monastery. For several years he was not allowed to say mass or to be a parish- priest, which he never did become.

He lived in Radomyśl with his aged mother, not in the presbytery, and did not receive a church annuity. He had constant financial difficulties, even court cases over taking bribes, arranging backing for money; in fact, he helped arrange visas to America, and thanks to him half of the neighborhood emigrated.

Despite this, or maybe because of this, in his native parts people respected and liked him. During the occupation he raised everyone's spirits by helping the partisans, giving patriotic sermons, in which he threatened the occupiers with fire and brimstone. Those who didn't like him called him a "soapbox orator" and a demagogue; and he really could carry away the congregation -- he used to stretch himself out on a cross during sermons, intoned loud joint prayers to the pealing of church bells.

No one knows by what channels the Kosińskis got to him. It wasn't very far from Sandomierz to Radomyśl, and they might have heard that he helped Jews. Here is what his biographer wrote about him:

" ... During the occupation Father Okoń was very active socially in the so-called Zasanie region; after being expelled from Tamobrzeg and the vicinity, the Jewish population was driven to several places of Zasanie. He organized a committee to help the displaced persons and was elected its chairman. The committee collected gifts, mostly in kind, and distributed them to the most needy.

He extended special care to two displaced persons: the 80-year-old doctor Reich of Rozwadów and his 75-year-old sister, a retired school teacher deported from Vienna, both of whom found a temporary haven in Radomyśl. His wards, however, seeing no hope for themselves, attempted suicide. The sister died, the old doctor was saved, but during the next transport he was shot and killed by a German policeman.

Another time Rev. Okoń took under his roof a Jewish family sent to him by acquaintances. The family had false papers bearing the surname Kosiński. Then, in a rented wagon the priest conveyed them to his acquaintances *in* Zasanie and found lodgings for them. This family survived the war."[2]

Father Okoń -- at least people in Dąbrowa said - allegedly took money from the Kosińskis, which would not be not surprising, for he never scorned money. He had baptismal certificates drawn up for them, but he could not hide them in his home he was too much in the "public eye." So he asked for the help of a few local resourceful and cunning peasants. Jozef Stępak, village administrator of Dąbrowa and Kępa, who had to know what was going on in "his" bailiwick. Władek Pamuła, village administrator of Wola Rzeczycka, had "pull" in the commune in Radomyśl, and it was he who got identification papers for the Kosińskis. Andrzej Warchoł just then was looking for a tenant to fill the apartment that had been vacated by the Liebeskinds.

The peasants did not dare to refuse their benefactor, the more so as he wouldn't take "no" for an answer. Besides, they were afraid, for the priest put the fear of God into them; he threatened them with hell, eternal damnation, reminded them that a good Christian helps his neighbors. He promised plenary indulgence.

And he didn't give any of them a cent, even Warchoł, who was risking the most and barely making ends meet. He was and remained poor; he never become rich, and neither did his children. From the Kosińskis he only collected rent, as he did from all of the people who leased apartments from him.

Father Okoń continued to be interested in them, especially in the first months, when it was not yet certain how they would be received. He often came to visit them on his bike and dropped in at the Warchołs', Migdałeks'. He queried them on how the village had received his charges. Was everything all right? Did he have to remind anyone of the Last Judgment and hell? Later, he stopped coming; in the last months of 1942 the Gestapo came for him, and it was only by a miracle that he avoided arrest and managed to hide somewhere in the vicinity until-almost the end of the war.

---

[2] T. Rek, *Ksiądz Eugeniusz Okoń,* LSW, Warsaw 1962, pp. 182-3

In Mr. Migdałek's opinion, Jurek Kosiński later immortalized the priest in his *Painted Bird* as one of the few positive characters. The priest in his novel -- like Okoń - is short (barely five-feet tall), plump, in a dusty, frayed cassock. Above all -- he is warm-hearted, kindly, always ready to help. He persuades one of the rustics to take the Boy in, then visits him and watches over him, invites him to church, as Father Okoń did the Kosińskis.

✳ ✳ ✳

"Though in 1942 Jurek was only nine years old" -- Mr. Andrzej Migdałek recalled – "he must have been made aware of his situation and of the danger hanging over not only his family but over the entire village. For he never ran out anywhere, never sneaked out, he didn't even have to be watched."

And he probably only went outside twice without the permission of his parents. Today it is hard to say how this could have happened. Where was Mrs. Kosiński? Katarzyna? Anyway, he and little Andrzej Migdałek ran off to the river San, to which the entire village was racing to see the enormous sheatfish caught by one of the peasants. But like everybody else, he stayed there for only a little while, looked, and returned home.

We can suppose that he was forgiven, for he sneaked out without permission one other time. What is more, not only with little Andrzej Migdałek but also with Henio, whom Katarzyna must have let out of her sight for a moment. They ran down to the nearby shallow stream, in which all of the kids used to wade and splash about during the summer and where little Andrzej learned to swim. Jurek and Henio were there for the first time, but they only stood and watched. Despite the heat, they didn't go into the water, nor did they undress like the other children; they stood there the whole time in their shirts and shorts. This time, however, when they returned home they got such a spanking that they never went out without permission again.

It was the worst in the winter -- Jurek loved winter sports. And like all of the Dąbrowa folks, he had skates -- wooden "hooks" that tied on to shoes with cords -- and a wooden sled with metal runners; he used to glide on the ice on this sled and support himself with a metal rod.

So once he entreated his mother, who let him go to the nearby frozen pond where all the local children used to skate. He went with little Andrzej, whom Mrs Kosiński liked -- he was quiet and sensible.

But they returned *very* quickly. Older kids, excellent skaters, boys from the next village, started to chase them, to bar their way and shout after Jurek: "Little Jew! Little Kike!" He got so scared that he wanted to come home right away.

But he forgot about this quickly and talked his mother into letting him go skating again, this time also with little Andrzej. Once again, they returned quickly, but this time they were really scared out of their wits, their hearts in their mouths. They were chased by older boys from Dąbrowa, headed by their ringleader, Świetlik, who today lives in the United States. They shouted at Jurek to drop his pants and show them his "bird" to prove that he was not circumcised! Little Andrzej Migdałek taunted Świetlik to show them his "bird" first. For everybody knew that he was a Jew, but a convert! This was true, and it so infuriated Świetlik that -- with his gang -- he jumped Jurek, threw him down on the ice, and started to pull down his pants.

Jurek defended himself desperately, struggled, covered himself with his hands, and -- above all -- yelled for all he was worth, literally squealed: *"Mame! Mame!"* Mr. Migdałek remembers this squeal to this day, for never before had he heard Jurek utter a single word in Yiddish.

He tried to help him, of course -- he pulled him by the hand, dragged him out from under his assailants, whom he punched and kicked! He was alone, however, and things might have ended badly had it not been for the sudden appearance of seventh-grader Edek Warchoł, the landlord's son, who was strong and almost grown up. Świetlik and his pals, who were all much younger than Edek, immediately took fright and scattered in all directions. Jurek, meanwhile, got up and ran home as fast as his legs could carry him.

And for a long time he had the willies. He eventually regained his aplomb, but he lost the desire to go skating.

* * *

In May 1943 Jurek - with his peers and Andrzej Migdałek - received First Holy Communion. Parish-priest Sebastiański made no trouble for young Kosiński, about whom he knew everything from Father Okoń, but even if he hadn't been told, Jurek's looks were a dead giveaway. Jurek looked almost the same, in his later years, except that his thick curly hair was cut short, almost to the scalp.

So like all of the other novitiates, Jurek must have attended catechism in the parish church in Wola Rzeczycka. He always left home with little Migdałek but returned alone. Andrzej, as he recalls, was quiet and diffident, he hated fights, but -- after all -- he was only nine years old. So after religious instruction, on the way home he stayed behind with his pals to play war, that is, throw stones at one another. Andrzej, of course, tried to get Jurek to play, but the latter always explained that he couldn't, that his parents had forbidden him to play with the local boys! He said good-bye and returned alone, even though Andrzej Migdałek called him a cry- baby and sissy. And only today does Mr. Migdałek understand Jurek's self-discipline, maturity. He understands his caution toward his peers.

After Holy Communion Father Sebastianski urged them to become altar boys, and they dared not refuse. They received surplices, bells, and became assistants to the older altar boys, but they served only during evening Masses, never at High Masses, to which they were not yet admitted.

During one Mass, when Jurek was standing before the altar, the older altar boys -- as boys will do -- started to poke each other with their elbows and titter. It was quite possible they were laughing at Jurek. After all, he was a Jew serving at Mass. Or perhaps he had tripped? Or had grown faint? He was frail, not as "athletic" as the village boys.

Like the Boy in *The Painted Bird*, Jurek did indeed suddenly fall down in front of the altar, drop the missal that he was supposed to hand to the priest. But he got up quickly, picked up the missal and handed it over.

He must have taken this very hard, but nothing really happened. He remained an altar boy, Father Sebastiański didn't admonish him or even mention this to him. He knew Jurek's situation, and that's why he always singled him out, made him an altar boy, an honor that was reserved only for the "better" boys -- clean, intelligent wide-awake.

Unlike the hero of *The Painted Bird*, Jurek was not thrown into a latrine. Neither did he lose his voice. Not then or in any other circumstances. Little

Migdałek and his sister played with him until April 1944, and for the whole time they spoke normally with each other.

* * *

Unlike his peers, however, Jurek did not attend the local four-grade elementary school; despite the fact that it was in the next barrack and was taught by Andrzej Migdałek's father. To say the truth, though, the school was rarely open; in the winter there was no fuel, in the summer the children had to help out in the fields, and the Germans were always summoning the teacher to assist in keeping various records, collecting levies. Sometimes classes were held, but without Jurek, who was taught by his father every day without fail. Jurek could play with the Migdałek kids or "hang" on the fence only until dinner, at which time his mother called him inside. After dinner the lessons began; they included English, in which Jurek already was quite fluent. Besides this, he was always sitting on the porch with his nose in a book. He read a lot, all of Sienkiewicz's *Trilogy,* for example; though Jurek wasn't even ten yet, he was very mature for his age.

Yet, he obviously hadn't stopped being a child, so it's no surprise that one time he broke down and opened up. One day when he was playing on the porch with little Ewa Migdałek, for no reason whatsoever he blurted out that his name wasn't Kosiński at all but Lewinkopf. He was a Jew from Łódź. The Weinreichs, grandparents on the distaff side, were owners of a leather goods factory, his mother always wore beautiful gloves ... He was circumcised, and that's why he couldn't go out to play with the other children...

Little Ewa, of course, repeated all of this to her parents, who immediately told "old man" Kosiński, mainly out of solicitude to prevent Jurek from saying "such things" again. On the same day the professor brought Jurek for a "showdown," more precisely had to drag him in by the ear. For "the Little Back Spider" resisted, kicking and screaming. He cried, sobbed, threw a tantrum. He shouted that he hadn't said anything -- Ewa had lied! She had thought up everything and now was blaming him!

Fortunately, the professor found a good way out of this situation; he said that Jurek had a crush on Ewa. She was his first love, and so he had wanted to impress her by telling a cock-and-bull story ...

In the opinion of Mrs. Ewa Dziadek, Jurek "got even" with her many years later in *The Painted Bird* by naming the girl whom the Boy falls in love with Ewa, who "deceives" him not only with her brother and father but also with a goat.

On the other hand, he really did like to impress people, show off, play the wit. To pretend to be grown up, worldly wise, tell jokes whose meaning he didn't understand. Only today do people wonder where on earth he could have heard them. Certainly not from his parents; who were very cultured, upright, and cared about his education. It's also hardly likely he heard them from Katarzyna. Though she was a simple woman, she was proper, dignified, hardly the type who would tell filthy jokes.

Mrs. Ewa Dziadek remembers one of them to this day. Jurek giggling all the time, once told how a soldier made a date with a virgin and asked her what he could treat her to. She said *ices,* which he bought for her, and in the end couldn't hold out any longer and said: "Maggie, am I going to go in on skates?"

After the "business" with little Ewa, for some time he was cross at the Migdałeks, gave them a wide berth, didn't go to their yard. He just hung on the fence, watching what was going on in the vicinity. Forest, marshes, railroad tracks, trains passing frequently on the way to the concentration camps. Farms of the closest neighbors, especially of the bird-fancier Lech Tracz, who most probably became the archetype of Lech from *The Painted Bird.*

During the occupation the original Lech was a teenager (born 1929), lived with his parents and brothers and sisters, and already then did not have all of his buttons. During childhood he had suffered meningitis, as a result of which he remained a big child, but he was liked by everybody -- he was gentle, even-tempered.

From his earliest years he loved the forest; he used to go there every morning and return in the evening. He went to watch and listen to the birds, which were and still are his passion, especially song birds -- goldfinches, canaries. He used to catch them in a snare of horse hair, seeds, hemp; he kept them for some time in cages that he wove himself, then let them go or sold them. He had many buyers -- in those days the children didn't have any toys. It was mainly for the children, as well as for himself, that he sometimes painted the birds with lime, for where could one get paint during the occupation? And like Lech from *The Painted Bird,* he would release them and then watch how the flock attacked them furiously.

Lech Tracz still lives in Dąbrowa, in a cottage hung with cages filled with birds, right opposite the now pulled down barracks in which the Kosińskis had lived. He is still drawn to the forest, but now goes there less often; he's well over sixty, recently broke both legs and gets around with difficulty. Since the death of his parents, he has lived alone, but his sister and her family built a house next to his cottage and take care of him.

* * *

The Kosińskis weren't the only Jews hiding out in Dąbrowa. For a year and a half the Migdałeks under their roof sheltered a Jewish brother and sister -- twelve- year-old Likla and six-year-old Jurek, who had identification papers and baptismal certificates made out in the name Małaczyński. For money they had been plucked out of the Cracow ghetto; they were the children of the lady friend of their aunt, a Jewess nee Mandelsztajn, married to one of the Migdałeks.

One day this aunt brought Lilka and Jurek to Dąbrowa without a word of warning. She explained that it was safer in the countryside, that the war was coming to an end. So the Migdałeks took them in for a time, they wanted to help, and besides - the aunt promised 500 zloty a month for their upkeep. That's not much, considering the risk, but for the Migdałeks it was a lot -- they were almost always on the verge of hunger; there wasn't much to buy for Mr. Migdałek's teacher's salary.

Meanwhile, neighboring Kępa, where Kosiński got his provisions, had very fertile land; there one could buy potatoes, vegetables, milk, and butter. Very expensive, but available.

The village must have noticed Lilka and her brother Jurek; after all, they used to go out into the yard, attended church, and they had very Semitic features, especially Jurek. Yet, the villagers pretended not to see them or the Kosińskis. Only the children would sometimes call out after them: "Jews! Little Kikes!" -- not only at the Mataczynskis but also at the little Migdałeks. The Kosińskis -- their nearest neighbors -- also must have noticed them, but despite this -- Jurek Kosiński continued to visit the Migdałeks.

The reason is that for a long time Dąbrowa remained a safe-haven. The Germans rarely dropped in here. Most often the so-called blue policemen -- peasants from Poznan province, speaking excellent Polish, who were later executed by the partisans. These policemen were not very zealous, however, they never looked in at the Migdałeks'. The Germans stationed in Zaklików and Rozwadów also rarely came by -- but they sometimes did. Mr. Andrzej Migdałek remembers the following incident as if it happened yesterday.

One day he was playing outside with his sister Ewa, Likla and Jurek, and also with Jurek Kosiński and little Henio, who was under the watchful eye of Katarzyna. Just then she had taken the little shaver to the fence for a "wee-wee," which took them about half an hour.

For, unlike other kids, little Henio didn't do wee-wee anywhere at all, without being bashful about his surroundings. Katarzyna always took him to the latrine or to the fence. She used to turn him around, undress and then dress him for a long time. Even in the summer he used to walk around, or rather waddle, in three pairs of trousers. The outer pair was thick -- fastened by a belt, the second -- thin, the third -- tight-fitting, like leotards. Under these pairs of pants were his undies, which had a lot of buttons.

And suddenly, just as Katarzyna was standing with him by the fence -- Mr. Andrzej Migdałek still vividly recalls -- around ten Germans with tin badges on their chests rode into the courtyard. They stopped and, without dismounting, asked his father whether he had any Jews left in his area. He had a weak heart and nearly swooned when he heard this, but by some miracle he managed to blurt out - he fortunately knew German - that they long since had been sent to Zaklików ...

In the meantime, the Germans - which is hard to believe - paid no attention at all to the children, though the looks of Jurek Kosiński and Małaczyński would have left no doubt in their minds.

Fortunately, Mrs. Migdałek also kept her cool. She appeared in the doorway and acting as though nothing was wrong - called the children inside for dinner. Of course, they all came running, but Jurek Kosiński and Henio's nanny at the fence became paralyzed with fear. However, the Germans seemed unaware of their presence. They just glanced around the yard and then galloped off.

After this incident, Andrzej Migdałek's father asked his aunt to take in Lilka and Jurek. For their presence not only threatened his children but also the Kosińskis hiding next-door. His uncle arrived immediately, but he took only Jurek, who was more Semitic in appearance and circumcised. He postponed the departure of Lilka -- she had contracted strong ulcerous pains, and in this situation, he was afraid to take her to another new place, which also wasn't easy to find. She remained in Dąbrowa for another several months and spent a total of one and a half years here. He took her when the man-hunts for partisans started here, a real hell. Right after the war, he learned that Lilka and Jurek had survived the occupation and had gone to Israel but contact with them was lost.

* * *

Karol Liebeskind, son of the local Jews who had run the saw-mill and whose apartment the Kosińskis had taken over, was also hiding out in the vicinity. Only the old Liebeskinds showed up at the assembly point; before this, they had taken their twenty-year-old Aryan-looking daughter to their aunt, who was married to a Pole and in whose home she survived. Twenty-four-year-old Karol, however, a law student with Semitic features, started to conceal himself in the vicinity, mainly in the woods.

Even before they went to Zaklików, his parents had begged neighbors and partisans to help their son, in so far as they were able, of course. So, the Home Army boys took him in, but not for long -- they scorned the "Yid" who, to say the truth, was unsuited for the partisans. He was a typical four-eyed intellectual, subtle and delicate. Then he went to the communist People's Army, out of the frying pan into the fire, so to speak; he messed around there for a while, but not for very long.

He most often wandered around in the vicinity of Dąbrowa, where the people liked the Liebeskinds, especially the old man, their employer; so they helped his son. The most help came from the Krawczyks and Jóźwiaks, in whose homes he spent the winter hiding behind the cupboard or in the cellar.

He usually slept in forest dug-outs, hay-stacks. He entered the village only at dusk, and in agreed upon places food and clean clothes were left for him in outhouses and barns.

Neither did he avoid the Migdałeks, who on his account got many grey hairs. He was visiting them one evening, when, all of a sudden, even though they had put out all of the lights, someone started pounding on the door and shouting in German. They quickly concealed Karol in the cellar and opened the door, but the unexpected visitor turned out to be the drunken German soldier who guarded the railroad bridge over the river San and who liked to tip the bottle and often ventured into the village for "drinking bouts"; people say that he even drank with the partisans. In his drunken stupor he quite often lost his way and went wherever his feet took him.

Another time Karol was in their home in the daytime -- his washed and deloused clothes had not yet dried out. Meanwhile, around noon a so-called penal expedition against partisans consisting of more than one hundred horse-drawn sleighs bearing German soldiers dressed in white protective coveralls and armed with machine guns drove up all around the barracks.

He was killed on 20 June 1944, just before the Russians came, when the sounds of the approaching front were already rumbling in the distance. He was sitting in a barn of one of the peasants, when - quite accidentally, Germans halted in the vicinity. The farmer warned Karol, who took off for the forest. But the Germans saw him, they fired and hit him in the thigh. Karol's nerves simply didn't hold out; he was also tipsy -- for, of late, brought to the edge of endurance by fear and the ordeals of his vagabond life, the cold, the lice -- he had taken a fancy to moonshine, of which there was no shortage in the village.

After he was caught, he didn't betray anyone; he kept saying that he was an English parachutist, and he knew the language perfectly. So, the German doctors decided to operate on him and took off his clothes. But, when they saw that he had been circumcised, they immediately put him to death with an injection of phenol, so that he would have a quick and painless death. Then, of course, the Germans summoned the village administrator, the entire village of Dąbrowa, who to a man maintained that they had never seen this person before, that they had no idea who he was and where he had come from. The war was ending, the

Germans long since had ceased to be what they were at the beginning, and they took no reprisals.

Karol was buried behind the shed of the nearest farm; only after several years did his sister, who had survived, move his remains to the local cemetery in Wola Rzeczycka, where she erected a tombstone. And she always comes here on All Souls' Day, lights candles, visits those who helped him the most - keeps in touch with them.

* * *

However, Dąbrowa remained relatively safe and quiet only for a short time. It was situated on the Rozwadów-Lublin railroad line, on which military trains went back and forth to the eastern front. So, like bees to honey, ever larger groups of partisans began to gather in the local forests, especially in Jankowo-Lipskie. The partisans started to blow up the military trains, hardly one of which could get through without encountering a mine. Mr. Migdałek remembers how, once day, he and Jurek Kosiński ran outside to watch the columns of fire from the exploding railroad cars. Most often on the railroad bridge over the river San, over which constant battles were beingfought.

For assistance to the partisans the Germans burned down and executed entire villages, among them nearby Lasoki, Kochany, Goliszowiec, Rzeczyca Długa, Kruszyna, Janiki. Few people managed to escape to the forest. The Germans conducted pacification operations, round-ups. Many times, panic broke out that once again trouble was afoot, and then everybody, including the Kosińskis, ran away to the forest with his cattle and belongings. They hid in outdoor cellars called pits.

The underground army here was quite diverse, but for the most part it was "red," "leftist," just like the vicinity, which before the war had showed leftist and even communist tendencies. The "white," Home Army forces, which predominated in Radomyśl, Rozwadów, Żabno, were much weaker and less numerous here. And in addition to the "Reds and Whites," there were also cut-throats and thugs, who slept during the day and at night robbed, stole and settled their scores.

And it was they, for what reason no one knows, who started to pay nightly visits to the Migdałeks. At first, they pretended to be partisans, they asked for maps of the vicinity, but soon dropped this masquerade.

They came in the night, pounded on the door and windows with their rifle butts, staggered in drunk, cursed loudly. One night they came when Mr. Migdałek had "gone begging," that is, in search of food to a family in nearby Dąbrówka Pniowska. They asked where and to whom he had gone, alleged that he had denounced them to the Germans, threatened that they would show him! They ostentatiously loaded their weapons, ransacked the apartment, though there wasn't anything valuable there expect a watch on a chain, which they took, of course.

Ewa and little Andrzej Migdałek fell ill as a consequence of each nightly "visit" -- they stammered, suddenly woke up in the night screaming, trembled with fear whenever someone knocked at the door.

In April 1944 the Migdałeks -- mainly for the sake of the children -- left Dąbrowa and went to their family in Rabka. Mr. Migdałek couldn't quit his job, however; so, his wife managed to get a certificate in the town office in Krasnik stating that they were being harassed by the partisans. And then the Germans allowed them to leave Dąbrowa perfectlylegally.

The Migdałeks feared new "visits," and so they departed in great haste and didn't even take leave of the Kosińskis - there was no time.

The town of Sandomierz before World War II. The Kosiński family was hiding here in the first years of the occupation of Poland.

A collection centre in Dąbrowa Rzeczycka, where Kosinski's father worked during the occupation

1946, Jurek Kosiński in Jelenia Góra, where he and his parents lived after the war.

The author, Joanna Siedlecka with Edward Warchoł, Andrzej's son, and Józef Szkutnik from Wola, Adam's son. They, among others, were the ones who told the author the story of the Kosiński family.

CHAPTER 6

The Professor's Little Son

Andrzej Warchoł and his wife, with whom the Kosińskis stayed, are no longer living. However, their children are alive: in neighboring Wola Rzeczycka -- their son Edward Warchoł (1927), who got married there. In Dąbrowa Rzeczycka -- in the place of the long since dismantled barracks -- their daughter Stefania Wołoszyn (1939) with her husband and children.

Edward Warchol in particular remembers the Kosińskis; Stefania Wołoszyn, called "Wołoszynka," knows them only from her parents' stories about them, and they talked about them often. When their father brought them from Radomyśl in the fall of 1942, the mother immediately started to cry.

"Jędrus, dear God, what have you done? Why, these are Jews! Do you want to cause the death not only of your children but of the entire village? They'll burn all of us alive! Do you know how long this war may still last?"

"Hush, Mary!" -- he reassured her - "everyone wants to live! Right now there's an empty flat, let them stay there! And they *have* children! Besides, could I refuse Father Okori? I even kissed his hand when I took leave of him!"

And though little Stefania was only three years old and Edzio only fourteen, he somehow managed to convince his wife. She was a *very* kindly person, obliging and sincere, and also deeply religious. Father Okoń chose a really ideal place for the Kosińskis -- another woman might not have agreed to take them in or soon there would have been conflicts, but with "Warchołka" this was simply impossible - she always patched things over, calmed everyone down.

Three flats had entrances from the side of the road, a field road but still a road. Three others - more private -- had entrances from the yard, and it was these they asked for, and were very happy when they got them.

"How can we ever repay you, Mary?" -- Mrs. Kosiński constantly asked Mrs.Warchoł.

"The most important thing is for all of us to survive" -- the latter responded.

Maybe the entire village wouldn't have been burned down, but the barracks surely would have been, for they didn't "turn in" their neighbor! Despite this, none of the tenants ever came to and raised Cain: what is he collecting rent for?

He's bringing misfortune not only upon himself!

"It can't be helped" -- people said --"they've piled in, let them stay, it's God's will!"

And Wiesia Bączkowska from flat number three had children even younger than the Kosińskis. What is more, her husband had brought them here from Warsaw, for it was supposedly safer in the country! Even though there were Jews right next door, did she ever say a word to Warchoł?

* * *

At first everything was all peaches and cream. They were nice, polite, paid on time, always with brand new bank notes. So people wondered, where do they get them from? They surely had resources -- gold? dollars? -- otherwise they wouldn't survive the occupation. Here, however, they at most could sell something for a tub of butter or sack of potatoes, for no one had money. They almost never left Dąbrowa, and when they did it was to go to Kępa or Wola, which were just as poor as Dąbrowa. Later, the professor started to work at the state purchasing center, but that place was visited only by locals, who also were by no means flush. Neither were the partisans, with whom the professor later maintained contacts. So they must have had someone on the outside.

The Jews were famed for their solidarity, and so it wasn't any surprise that they had taken in Henio, but people also whispered that it was for him that they had "gotten money... Katarzyna, who used to quarrel with Mrs. Kosiński over the latter's coldness to Henio, sometimes didn't hide this in her anger. Though they lived under one roof, one could sense that they were not one family, of which the Kosińskis made no secret, despite the fact that Henio, and especially Katarzyna, improved the

Kosińskis' "bad" appearance. Katarzyna fearlessly moved about the farmyard, made trips to the village -- she had typically Polish looks; Henio on the other hand -- typically Semitic features, but blond hair, a light skin, chubby face and figure.

They must have had money, they bought food, and a lot of it, for there were five of them -- three adults, two children. Mrs. Kosiński right away asked Mrs. Warchoł if she would be willing - for additional money, of course - to clean her flat, for she wasn't up to it herself. Mrs. Warchoł refused - she had a farm, a small child, and whoever heard of a landlady cleaning a tenant's flat, especially of a tenant whom she was harboring?

Mrs. Warchoł then approached neighbors, "Traczka" and "Stelmaczka"; they willingly agreed - for them every penny counted. Soon Mrs. Kosiński permanently hired Labina of Dąbrowa; the woman had small children, she was a renter and wanted to make some money.

Stefania Labina (1910) still lives in Dąbrowa and remembers that she used to go to the "Kusińskis" day after day. She did everything -- scrubbed the floors, cooked, milled grain, baked bread, prepared the reception for Jurek's First Holy Communion, and in those days washing was a real chore -- one had to carry water from the well, heat it, rub clothes on the washboard, hang them on the line, press them with an old-fashioned "heater" flat-iron.

Mrs. Kusiński on the other hand -- like a real lady -- only busied herself with the children. Or she did up her hair, blackened her eyebrows, drew dress patterns on sheets of paper (always with a mandarin collar to hide her swollen thyroid gland), which were then sewn for her by Stanisława Bogucka of Rzeczyca Okrągła.

Bogucka also made clothes for "old man" Kusiński and for Jurek and Henio, who grew out of everything, since one couldn't buy clothes in a store!

* * *

Ferdynand Stępak (1930) distinctly remembers "old man" Kosiński, who often used to drop by to see his father, the late Jozef Stępak, village administrator of Dąbrowa and Kępa under the German occupation. Kosiński used to help his father in his duties -- keeping books, figuring levies, taxes. He wrote letters and petitions in German, counseled him in various official matters.

In exchange for this, Mrs. Stępak always filled up a bag of "life" for him -- butter, cheese, cream. Mr. Stępak, on the other hand, who was pleased with the help he had received, always threw in something from himself, in secret from his wife, who, like a woman, constantly feared that there wouldn't be enough left over for herfoursome.

The professor also often bought "life" from neighbors in Kępa, and all of them sold food to him cheaper, reduced the price. Only in the little store in Dąbrowa, where they sold rationed bread and marmalade from beets, did he pay the official price, just as for wood from the forest. From the peasants, only for "as much he deemed sufficient," for he was a PROFESSOR, a "scholar," "highly educated," practically a tsar and a god!

"The peasant was poor, ignorant, without schooling. An illiterate" -- said Stępak. – "He felt humble before the professor, as he did before a doctor and a priest."

Despite the fact that he was a "Yid"; and Jews had always been treated rather well here, but nonetheless a bit contemptuously, patronizingly.

They were proud that they were concealing such a Jew! Not a tenant, not a shopkeeper, but a PROFESSOR, who probably jabbered in all of the languages known to man!

"Of course they were afraid, they lived -- Stępak recalls – "in 'fear and trembling' -- they knew what they were risking." However, it never entered anyone's head to "turn them in." "Here" -- he emphasized – "there were no 'skunks', double- dealers or any Judases, rouges, dogs -- no traitors, pure and simple. Not like in Rozwadów, for example, where someone promised to take the Jews driven to Zaklików over the river San -- and then an escape to Vienna! Several of them, petrified with fear, believed him, paid him money, and he drowned them all!"

* * *

Only the late Adam Szkutnik of Wola once had the cheek to make rather innocent mockery of the professor's Jewishness. It was right after Stalingrad, when the Germans were starting to lose, and that's why, here at least, the Germans started to tum a blind eye to many things. And so the peasants, on the sly, of course, started to slaughter swine, even though such an act carried a death sentence; they removed the earmarks from the larger specimens and placed them on young pigs reared in haystacks, in forest hiding-places.

They also sold fresh meat and finger-sausage surreptitiously, though more and more openly as the occupation neared its end. Even the Germans stationed here used to buy pork from Szkutnik, as his son recalls, and not only for themselves but also before visits by their families from the Reich, where rationing had been imposed and where there was hunger. They sometimes even took half a calf, joints of pork, sausages.

One of the best customers was also professor Kosiński -- he had "money" and gold: bracelets, rings, gold coins, with which he paid for the meat. He bought a lot and often, mostly sausages, veal and beef, pork very rarely, though he emphasized that since a long time he had been eating everything! But he bought mainly for his wife and the children, and they preferred lean meat!

One day, when there was only pork, he started to make a fuss, he didn't like the piece that had been set aside for him. Meanwhile, Szkutnik wanted to complete the transaction as quickly as possible -- one month earlier a woman neighbor had killed a swine for a funeral reception, but someone "stooled on her," and she was sent to the Majdanek concentration camp. So he lost his cool; and even though there were other customers there, he yelled:

"Make up your mind, it doesn't have trichinosis! The war is still going on and you're picking and choosing, do you want to eat Kosher food?"

Everyone laughed. Kosiński also laughed, but he didn't say anything, he grabbed the piece that had been put aside for him, took his leave, and went out.

Mr. Stefan Kochan (1922), today a retired official from Tarnobrzeg, comes from Rzeczyca Okrągła, and during the occupation he worked with professor Kosiński in the state purchasing center in Dąbrowa. He also visited the professor several times in his home, in the barrack, invited for a game of chess, which the professor loved, but had no one to play with. Mr. Kochan was one of the few who knew how to play; in the neighborhood he was regarded as a "learned man" -- he had finished three forms of grammar-school! So he wasn't surprised at the authority which the professor enjoyed -- educated, intelligent, well-informed about politics -- he had maps, a long pointer, with which he showed the movements of German and Allied forces and predicted the development of the military situation.

And from the visits to the professor's home he remembers the perhaps overly numerous holy pictures hanging on the walls. Jesus, the Mother of God, the Holy Family with Child. Very dusty, with cobwebs on them, as though they had been hanging there for a long time. Except for them -- everything spick-and-span, all tidied up, everything in its place.

But best of all he remembers the reception on the occasion of Jurek's First Holy Communion, which took place in May 1943. The professor invited him, because Mr. Kochan -- as the only person in the vicinity -- had a camera. A "Kodak" accordion-type, which he had bought for money earned when he had been called to serve in the so-called young men's labor construction brigades for the Germans. Kosiński asked for pictures of Jurek, and Mr. Kochan used up a whole roll of film; but since he was just learning how to take pictures, they didn't turn out too well. He gave all of the pictures to the professor, but unfortunately, he destroyed the negative.

He took pictures during the reception after Holy Communion, which -- he admits -- made an impression on him; he still remembers it vividly. It has become a normal event only of late, but at that time -- in Dąbrowa at least -- no one had ever heard of anything like this. The reception was arranged by Mrs. Kosiński and not only for Jurek but also for all of the children taking Holy Communion with him!

Benches were set up for them in the courtyard all around the church, fresh pancakes were served, and especially -- mugs of hot, fragrant COCOA with whipped cream! This was the occupation, there was poverty, almost hunger; an elderly, lonely local woman had even starved to death. There were many day- laborers without their own piece of land to till, who hired themselves out to richer farmers.

Mr. Edward Madurski, who also took Holy Communion at that time, remembers, for example, that right after the ceremonies he had to hurry off to the farmer for whom he worked, on Sundays as well.

So it is hard to imagine what an impression the COCOA made, which -- it's a shame to confess -- eclipsed the Holy Communion itself and became the sensation of the day! Neither the children nor the adults had ever tasted such an exotic beverage! The adults didn't even taste it then -- it was only for the children.

People also gave the professor's wife the once-over, since she now appeared in public for really the first time. She almost never left the confines of the farmyard, except to go to church on Sunday, but she stood in the corner and quickly returned home. The women, especially, were interested in the lady who even in "safekeeping" was unable to do without cleaning women, seamstresses, nannies, and servants. They commented on her shocking appearance here. Her makeup was very garish -- shaved eyebrows lined with a pencil, painted lips, red polish on her fingernails. A stylish, short outfit.

For a long time, people talked not so much about the Holy Communion itself as about the reception. They wondered how the Kosińskis had managed to acquire such luxuries as cocoa and fingernail polish. Were these from prewar stocks? If not, who provided them with these things and from where?

Mr. Jan Pamuła (1926), now a retired engineer from Stalowa Wola, a native of Rzeczyca Okrągła, was regarded as someone from a better family. His father, Sylwester Pamuła, worked on the railroad, which was a government job; he earned 200 zloty a month and could afford the luxury of educating his son.

Even before the war Janek Pamuła had completed six grades of elementary school; and since he was supposed to continue his education, during all of 1943 and 1944 he used to go to professor Kosiński twice a week for lessons. The professor covered the first two forms of grammar-school with him, and after the war Janek was able to enter the third form of the grammar in Rozwadow and had no problems; he was a good student and later became the first person in his locality to obtain a secondary-school certificate and graduate from college.

He was brought to the Kosińskis by his aunt Stanisława Bogucka, who sewed for them; the professor was also teaching her son Rysek. Lessons obviously carried a risk, so the professor only gave them to children of trusted people who had been recommended to him.

He took payment in kind -- potatoes, eggs, butter. He taught all subjects, and one day he even gave Janek an anatomy lesson on "how children are made" that wasn't in the curriculum and at that time was a taboo subject. He was a great teacher -- Mr. Pamuła remembers him well. He knew a lot, was able to convey his knowledge, but sometimes he became annoyed, grit his teeth, shouted: "I already said that!"

Then the professor's wife, whom her husband called "Kosia," as though poking fun at their last name, would break in. She calmed things down, explained, pacified; she was clearly in charge in this house, she maintained discipline. She meddled in everything -- she had graduated from grammar-school, had a secondary-school certificate, played the piano, which she often mentioned. She was well-read, intelligent, eloquent, spoke beautiful Polish, without any trace of an accent, as did her husband and son.

Jan Pamuła remembers Jurek Kosiński, of course, who was close-rapt, serious, mature for his age. And with big, coal-black eyes, really "bewitching." Intelligent, well-read -- not only his father but also his mother worked with him. During one lesson she said she was taking him through expressions needed in discussion, such as "I don't deny that," "I don't negate that," "I will compromise" -- even though he was only ten years old.

He also remembers an event that shows what great authority the professor enjoyed here. During one of the lessons a peasant from Dąbrowa came running in -- his child had fallen seriously ill and he had no money for a doctor.

The doctor from Radomyśl, to whom Dąbrowa used to go for treatment (in rare cases, of course), was of Jewish origin -- which everyone knew -- but he was assimilated, married to a Polish woman. The peasant in all likelihood had come to the professor as "the wisest person in the village," but perhaps he also thought that Jews, like Jews, surely knew each other, which was not improbable - for the Kosińskis had come from Radomyśl, from Father Okoń.

And he was right, for they did know each other. Mrs. Kosiński immediately wrote a letter to the doctor recommending their neighbor's child. The peasant quickly grabbed the letter, thanked them, arranged for a cart to take him to Radomyśl, and everything ended happily.

$$* \ * \ *$$

Mrs. Wiesława Bączkowska, the Kosińskis neighbor from the barrack, died recently, but her son Zbigniew (1940), a physical education teacher and coach, is still living. Though he was only a child during the occupation, he remembers a lot, mostly from stories he heard from his mother.

Before the war they lived in Warsaw. In the spring, the father -- out of concern for the safety of his wife and children -- brought them to his mother's parts, to Dąbrowa Rzeczycka, and settled them in Warchoł's barrack.

He was a captain in the Home Army (pseudonym "Zbyszek"), deeply involved in the underground -- Khedive, instruction in diversionary actions, explosives. He was killed in the Warsaw Uprising; Tomasz Strzembosz mentions him in *Storm Units of the Warsaw Underground 1939-1944.*

The mother had studied agriculture in college; she was intelligent, well-read, came from Warsaw, yet her relations with the Kosińskis, even though they were all intellectuals, were correct but not friendly. Though they were Jews, were in hiding, and she understood their situation, despite this -- though it is hard to believe -- she sometimes envied them!

For her husband, involved up to his ears in the underground, visited her rarely -- the trip was risky. She was constantly in fear for his safety and had to contend with life on her own -- feed, clothe and bring up two small sons; the youngest was born in Dąbrowa in 1943.

She even rented a small piece of land, tilled it with Stasia Rybakówna, a girl from the neighborhood, who for a few extra zloty also helped her to look after the children. But despite this help, Wiesława Bączkowska lost so much weight that she weighed hardly seventy pounds and was always tired.

For potatoes and milk, she sold all her dresses, jewelry, gold and silver rubles brought by her husband's family from exile in Siberia. She complained about the local peasants, who -- with no regard for her situation -- mercilessly skinned her alive, demanding a gold earring or bracelet for a tub of butter or a piece of meat.

She envied Mrs. Kosiński her resourceful, caring and devoted husband, thanks to whom she didn't have to worry about what to give the children to eat tomorrow, bargain with the peasants, slave in the fields.

She also envied them their fine furniture; hers was flimsy, put together by a local carpenter. Above all, she envied them their rather large library; her Warsaw flat had been completely burnedout.

At first, she asked Mr. Kosiński several times for neighborly help, but she soon stopped asking. Mrs. Kosiński was perhaps jealous of the young, pretty and single female neighbor, and never would allow it. Her husband has no time, he is not going to Kępa or Wola, he cannot run the risk, etc. Even though he used to go out every day -- they didn't show themselves off, but lived a normal occupational life like everyone else. And they had found an exceptionally safe place. The Germans rarely dropped in here; they only had a sentry post at the station and on the bridge over the river San and were mainly concerned with hunting down partisans.

Despite this, one day Mrs. Kosiński came running over to Bączkowska's place in tears, all of a dither, with a grievance. "We're in hiding!" -- she sobbed. -- But you told your children that we're Jews! They'll tell the wrong person and a tragedy will result!"

"And mother" -- Zbigniew Bączkowski recalls – "actually did talk about them with Stasia, with father when he came, and it's hard to keep secrets in a small flat. So one day when I went to their place to borrow a book, right out of the blue I said: "And I know that you are Jews!"

Mother, of course, reassured Mrs. Kosiński as much as she could, she pacified the situation. That she could be sure that nothing threatened them from her family's side. And Dąbrowa knows anyway, but its residents also are not to be feared. "She knows these people well," she said, "and maybe they are greedy and if they can -- they'll skin you alive, but that's all. It wouldn't enter their minds to resort to blackmail or denounce anyone. She could sleep peacefully and thank the fates for casting her in such a place!"

"In moments of nervous collapse, fatigue" -- Zbigniew Bączkowski recalls – "mother always was full of bitterness against father. He had left her alone with small children, he risked his life, while others, like the Kosińskis, lived comfortably, didn't give a thought to getting involved, even though they were in their prime!"

For father, among whose tasks was to establish Home Army cells, had also tried to enlist the professor -- he had met him on his visits to Dąbrowa, had talked with him about politics, about the military situation.

At first the professor agreed, but later he wiggled out of it -- that was the end of it! Bączkowski didn't hold this against him, he had been refused before, for not everyone wanted to be in the underground.

"Mother, however, deep in her heart did hold this against them, especially after father's death in the Uprising. The more so as when he was fighting and was killed, when she went in search of his grave, they were greeting the Red Army men with flowers. They gave a festive supper for them -- the din of the merrymaking resounded throughout the entire barrack."

In view of this, could she maintain contacts with them? She even stopped going over to them to borrow books, whose lack she felt sorely, and so she used to send her son, and this is why he remembered their library. Only sometimes she talked with Henio -- she liked him very much, for he was "worse," less loved, it was obvious that he wasn't theirs.

* * *

Jan Szkutnik of Wola, Jurek Kosiński's contemporary, remembers that not only he but all the local boys, such as Mietek Tracz, Maniek Krawczyk, Władek Papka, were very much interested in the professor's little son. But they had no contacts with him, for he hardly ever went out of the enclosure, his parents wouldn't allow it.

They could only observe him from afar, when he was hanging on the fence, playing ball in the yard or with Miśek, the Warchołs' merry, obedient dog, adored by everybody.

Jurek reminded him of an ugly black bird, an unsightly black bird. With black, fiery eyes. With black, curly, closely cropped hair.

He was always dressed in his "Sunday best," wearing either sandals or shoes, in the summer -- funny short pants; while they, even during the biggest heat waves, paraded around in long trousers, barefooted or in wooden clodhoppers.

However, all of them were just dying to see what his circumcised "bird" looked like, which -- as they had heard -- all Jews had. No one knew what this was, what it looked like. And they had an irresistible urge to check this out, for they would never get another chance like this!

So they hid behind the fence, but he never peed like they, anywhere at all, bold as brass. He always ran into the latrine, and so they thought of a way!

As soon as he went in, they threw in "fire-bombs" -- empty tin cans filled with carbide. They obviously thought that, frightened by the report and fire, he would run out with his trousers and underpants down! But even though they flushed him out of there several times in this way, he always managed to hold up his pants in his fist, and they didn't see a thing!

But they noticed that he sometimes used to sneak out of the compound and run off to the meadow, from where one had a better view of the railroad tracks on which the trains passed by, the biggest local attraction. And it was here that they "nabbed" him, threw him down on the ground, and started to pull down his pants. He defended himself ferociously, struggled, screamed for all he was worth, and they were just a hairs breadth from finally seeing the circumcised "bird"!

As if out of spite, however, just at that moment Stanisław Rybak, a neighbor, was passing by. If only local boys had been engaged in a brawl, he wouldn't have paid any attention to them. But he spotted the "professor's little son," heard his cries, and so he grabbed a stick, came after them, and sent them running off in all directions. That's not all. He ran over to the Kosińskis to tattle; for Jurek didn't know these boys, didn't know where they lived; thanks to Rybak, on that very same day he made the rounds with his father and "fingered" those who had assaulted him. Jan Szkutnik clearly remembers their visit.

"Szkutnik" -- the professor cried from the doorstep (he called the peasants by their last name, while they always addressed him as "professor"!). "Your son has harmed my boy!"

"My father gave me such a caning that after that I gave the 'professor's little son' a wide berth, as did my chums, who also got a good licking.

But despite this, we all felt sorry for him."

Even though he had a learned father, a mother with painted fingernails, a maid. A reception on the occasion of his First Holy Communion. English lessons. A ball, books, supposedly even a globe! He just sat there on the porch, ate sausage and veal, drank cocoa.

Supposedly he was a professor's little son, but to tell the truth -- he was a poor, miserable whippersnapper!

He couldn't leave the compound, swim in the river, follow the cows, couldn't go to the forest, throw "smoke-bombs," bake potatoes in a campfire.

He used to just hang there on the fence, watching over his "bird," which no one could see.

So when the bomb-shell hit many years later, when he wrote *The Painted Bird,* I take it, they at first thought that it might have been about "this"? After all, there had been so many fights, to-dos, scuffles over his "bird"!

But no -- it was about the crows of Lech Tracz.

CHAPTER 7

Professor Kusiński

Stanisław Miętus of Wola (1907) clearly remembers professor "Kusiński" -- he worked with him under the Germans in the state purchasing center in Dąbrowa, where local peasants used to bring their levies of grain and potatoes. The store- keeper and his assistants, one of whom was Miętus, weighed, sorted, loaded, while professor "Kusiński" kept the books, issued receipts, sat behind a desk, like a lord.

Goodness gracious, that he was a Jew, like his wife and "kid," everyone knew, of course, but pretended not to know, not to see. They didn't "stool" on him to the Germans -- admittedly they are Israelites, but they are people, too, aren't they? It would have bothered one's conscience, and how could one live after that?

They also knew, of course, what they were risking. The Germans didn't fool around, they didn't hesitate to bum down entire villages. They had burned down Goliszowiec, Kruszyna, Janiki, Świdry, Rzeczyca Długa. Mainly on account of help to the partisans, but it also could have been for helping Jews!

So they were angry at him for being too audacious. He sauntered around the neighborhood in broad daylight, on Sundays took his family to the church in Wola, where Germans also used to come, attend the services, take communion. As if that wasn't enough, he took a job in the state purchasing center, where Germans also used to drop in often!

The more so as "the wolf wasn't at his door," and they paid peanuts at the center. People used to carry out a second salary in their pockets, trouser legs, pants filled with rye, wheat, potatoes. "Kusiński," however, was too exposed to view for this; besides, he was in the office, behind a desk.

People racked their brains why had he gone there? Was he tempting fate?

Was he bringing disaster upon himself, the Warchołs, the entire village?

* * *

Engineer Adam Latawiec (1922) of Gdansk, now retired, a native of Wola Rzeczycka, and Stefan Kochan of Rzeczyca Okrągła also worked with the professor in the state purchasing center in Dąbrowa, but in the office. They wrote out receipts for the peasants entitling them to buy vodka, fats, some durable consumer goods. They drew up summary lists, in which the professor was an ace -- in the blink of an eye he added up long columns of numbers without a mistake.

The head of the purchasing center, a certain Treczko, called "Theczka" because of the way he pronounced his 'r's', talked him into taking a job here. Treczko was supposedly a stock broker from Gdynia, and heaven only knows how he ended up here; he was completely out of place in this god-forsaken hole. Handsome, elegant -- in riding-breeches, always wearing a tie. Intelligent, bright, he liked to talk with the professor about politics.

Messrs. Kochan and Latawiec, who then were young country boys, had latched onto jobs in the purchasing center just to get "papers," a stamp of being employed that would protect them from being deported to Germany for forced labor. When there was an exceptionally large number of deliveries, they worked around the clock and with shovels, for nothing could be wasted. Sometimes, even partisans from the forest were called in to help; they came during the night, loaded, and took their cut -- they had to eat, too.

They wondered about the professor, who -- on account of his age -- was not in much danger of deportation for work in Germany, and yet had decided to work here of his own free will. He earned little, but -- in their opinion -- risked a lot. For everyone knew he was a Jew, that he was in hiding. He also didn't have the best appearance, though not as bad as his wife's and son's, but none the less. And though he tried to blend in, dress sloppily, he didn't look like a local but like an intellectual, who provoked the question -- what is he doing here?

Meanwhile, gendarmes from nearby Zaklików and from somewhat more distant Rozwadów often used to drop in to the purchasing center. They talked mainly with Treczka, but they snooped around everywhere -- in the office, in the yard.

When one of the store-rooms burned down, as many as ten of them came and wrote up a report. They talked with Treczka; one of them even said something to Kosiński, who answered in such beautiful and fluent German that the gendarme just stood there stock-still -- how does he know the language so well? Who is he? What is he doing here? Kosiński became ghastly pale, his knees turned to rubber, but he answered something and apparently squirmed out of the situation, for the German stopped being interested in him and rode off with his companions.

Another time an event took place that Mr. Kochan still clearly remembers. One day he was sitting in the office with Adam Latawiec and professor Kosiński, when all of a sudden one of the gendarmes from Zaklików burst in. They usually went around in pairs, they feared the partisans, of whom there were more and more. But this time one of them came alone, but with a dog -- a wolf-hound. He didn't even ask for Treczka, didn't look at Kochan or Latawiec, but went straight up to the professor. In a sharp tone he asked him something in German, but Mr. Kochan doesn't know what it was -- he didn't know the language. Kosiński turned ashen, was struck dumb, didn't say anything, just lowered his head until his chin was almost touching the desk. The German, meanwhile, for the whole time kept his hand on his pistol holster. Mr. Kochan, petrified with fear, expected a shot to ring out any second, but the gendarme stood there for a while longer and then suddenly left. Kosiński waited for some time, and then, even though it was still a few hours to quitting time, ran out without saying a word. They thought he would never come back, but he returned on the next day as if nothing had happened and didn't even mention the "incident." He continued to work in the purchasing center until 1944, until the front neared, until the time of "lawlessness."

People often wondered, why didn't the gendarme shoot? He was probably afraid - he was alone. But why didn't he become interested in Kosiński later? What did he really want from him?

One can say that Kosiński had incredible luck with the Germans. He always got out of seemingly hopeless situations safe and sound.

Once he came within a hair's breadth of getting killed in Kępa. He was walking down the road with Stępak and Warchoł, when suddenly a britzka pulled up alongside them -- one of the local peasants was driving, and his passenger was Fuldner himself, head of the Zaklików military police! The very person who had ordered the execution -- at a wedding reception -- of lord and lady Horodyński, owners of the beautiful, rich Zbydniów estate, and their guests -- a total of 21 people, for which atrocity he was later executed by the underground.

He quickly jumped down from the britzka and came up to them. "What are you doing? Where are you going?" -- he asked.

"I just bought some oats and now I'm going home" -- truthfully explained Warchoł who spoke a little German.

"And you?" -- Fuldner suddenly addressed Kosiński, examining him suspiciously. -- "You, you *Jude! Jude!*"

And he took a pistol out of his pocket and aimed in Kosiński's direction.

"He's no *Jude,* he's a Pole, a professor who teaches our children!" – Warchoł quickly replied.

"Yes, a Pole, a professor, he came from the city!" -- Stępak, who also knew a little German, backed him up.

"A professor?" -- Fuldner said in surprise. -- Then what is he doing here? Why isn't he teaching? Why isn't he in school? He's a *Jude!*"

Kosiński on the other hand, who spoke fluent German, couldn't utter a single word in his defense, he just stood there paralyzed with fear.

Warchoł and Stępak were sure that Fuldner would blow Kosiński's brains out. He kept looking at him suspiciously, aiming the pistol at him the whole time. But he finally put his pistol away, climbed into the britzka without a word, and drove away. He apparently had been afraid to shoot -- he was alone, among Poles, close to the forest, maybe full of partisans? The Germans were cautious -- they rarely ventured into the heart of the village, let alone into the forest, and when they did they sent a unit armed to the teeth and on motorcycles.

But why did Fuldner, head of the local Gestapo, not later take an interest in someone whom he regarded as a *Jude,* someone he had wanted to kill? Why didn't he order a man-hunt for him? Judging from the crime in Zbydniów, one can hardly say that Fuldner was a good German.

Ferdynand Stępak of Kępa in tum remembers an even more miraculous event. On Sundays the professor with his wife and son sometimes used to drop in to his father's house on their way back from the church in Wola. One time they only went into the kitchen and sat down at the table, when all of a sudden Germans stationed in Kępa, who guarded the railroad bridge over the river San, drove into the yard.

The professor only managed to cry out: "Remember that we know each other!" But Stępak and his wife couldn't utter a word out of fear, they were completely struck dumb.

However, the Germans only went into the kitchen, asked Stępak something, stayed a while, and then left. They did glance at the terrified Kosińskis, but -- though it is hard to believe -- showed no interest in them whatsoever! Even though the appearance of Mrs. Kosiński and Jurek left no doubt.

Afterwards, village administrator Stępak always maintained that the Germans simply trusted him and no longer inquired into who his guests were. It probably never entered their heads that, since there had been no Jews here for a long time, some of them, like on a Sunday afternoon picnic, would be sitting here in the village administrator's kitchen.

✻ ✻ ✻

The Kosińskis also emerged whole and unscathed from all the patrols, man-hunts, pacification operations launched by the Germans in retaliation for the stepped-up partisan raids, mainly against the transports to the eastern front.

Somehow, they were always warned in time, managed to escape, hide -- in the cellar under the kitchen or in the outdoor cellar, called the "piit" in which vegetables and potatoes were kept.

For instance, Mr. Jan Pamuła recalls one day in January 1994 when he came to the professor's for his usual lessons; he had just put his school bag on the floor when one of the neighbors rushed in -- from the Warchołs? Jóźwiaks? - and shouted: "Germans!" Kosiński quickly hid behind the wardrobe in the parlor, Mrs. Kosiński, Jurek and Henio with his nanny scurried down the ladder to the cellar. They had hardly slammed the door shut when the Germans burst in, to be precise, Polish-speaking Silesians wearing German uniforms.

"Where is the master of the house?" -- they shouted.

"I haven't the foggiest, I came looking for him myself, they sent me from the state purchasing center" -- he whispered and a drop of sweat trickled down his back out of terror. After a while he became weak in the knees, but he got hold of himself, started to scrape his feet on the floor. For Kosiński suddenly moved, the wardrobe made a sound, and in the cellar, Henio began squeal, but was immediately silenced.

Fortunately, the Silesians didn't hear anything; in any event, they went out and didn't come back.

The Kosińskis waited out one of the operations in Jan Pamuła's house. Somehow the professor had learned that something was afoot in Dąbrowa, so he asked Jan's father to keep him "on ice" for a few days - Rzeczyca Okrągła was way off the beaten track. Sylwester Pamuła agreed - after all, Kosiński was teaching his son, had become friendly with his sister, Stanisława Bogucka, nee Pamuła, who sewed for them.

So he hid out at the Pamułas' -- with Jurek and Henio, of course -- for a few days. Bogucki's uncle even drove them there and back in a cart, because it was quite a way. While they were there Mrs. Pamuła prepared better dinners, Mr. Pamuła served vodka, after all, they were not ordinary guests!

One of the larger operations took place in the summer of 1943 -- the pacification of villages suspected of assisting the partisans. Many men were arrested, and the villages of Gwizdów, Kochany, Goliszowiec were burned to the ground. Every person who hadn't managed to escape to the forest perished. Though Dąbrowa wasn't the most "pro-partisan," an attack could have been expected at any time.

Ferdynand Stępak of Kępa remembers that it was then that the professor had rushed over to them and asked his father to keep him "on ice" -- the Germans are coming to Dąbrowa! Mrs. Kosiński, Jurek and Henio with his nanny ran to the forest with the women, Kosiński and Warchoł -- into the underbrush along the river, but at the last minute the former decided that this was too poor a hide-out.

Stępak was quaking with fear -- he had four small children, was the village administrator, was responsible for the entire village. Yet, he could not refuse Kosiński, he didn't want him to be caught -- for otherwise, Stępak would have been held accountable for having a Jew in "his" area, a Jew whom he did not "turn in" to the Germans.

He quickly hid Kosiński in the attic, where hay was being dried out at that time. Kosiński stayed up there for some time, and the village administrator's children carried food up to him. But he soon started to complain that he was suffocating, fainting, for it was stifling, hot -- the roof was too low, there was no window, and the odor of the hay was really getting to him! So Stępak told him to come down from the attic and hid him in the garden behind the house, in high, thick bean fields.

And even though the entire village had run off to the forest, Stępak stayed at home; after all, he was the village administrator. He just instructed his wife to cook up some chicken soup, leave some rationed vodka on the table. When the Germans poured into the yard, he politely invited them inside to table and treated them.

"They stuffed themselves, drank, lavished praise on father" -- his son recalls.

-- "As the village administrator is, so is the village!" - they said.

It looked as though everything would turn out well, but two of them needed to have a pee and went out into yard, right into the bean fields, two steps away from Kosiński! And they stood there for a long time, pulling up bean stalks and laughing. Stępak, paralyzed with fear, just sat there expecting the worst. Fortunately, Mrs. Stępak kept her cool; she grabbed a basket of wet wash, ran into the yard, and started to string up clothes-lines, put basins here and there, make a commotion to chase the Germans back into the house, in which she finally succeeded.

Later Kosiński related that they stood just a couple of steps from him, and he nearly fell under the earth with fear. For probably the first time his nerves couldn't hold out, he wanted to get up and run, but with the last remnants of his strength he got pulled himself together.

They also saved their skins during the operation in July 1944, just before the Russians arrived, when the retreating Germans had left behind a division of "Vlasov men" -- Kalmucks, with round faces and slanted eyes. Nearly all the residents of Dąbrowa had run off into the forest, where they camped out for at least a few days. Some of them were not able to get away in time, however. Franciszek Krawiec, for one, hid himself in the "pit" -- the cellar in the yard.

"Drunk, swaying on their feet" -- he told – "they even started to shoot there, so I had to crawl out!"

They caught him, told him to run to the people, get them to come out of the forest, otherwise they would put everything to the torch -- smoke the partisans out of the forest. He ran up to the forest, shouted at the top of his voice, but no one even poked his nose out, of course. Despite this, they didn't do anything to him, didn't burn down the forest, they just plundered the village -- robbed the food from the pits, turned the cottages upside down, including the barrack, in which the Kosińskis lived. They smashed in the windows, which for a long time after that were covered with paste-boards.

To tell the truth, they treated Dąbrowa rather kindly -- no fatalities, just devastation. But in Rzeczyca Okrągła they raped the women. They burned down almost all of Rzeczyca Długa, and everyone who didn't manage to run away perished.

They had been stationed here in the vicinity for a long time, in Rzeczyca Okrągła, among other places, at the Pamułas'. And, oh wonder of wonders -- they behaved themselves; they didn't undertake any actions on their own. They moved out only on the orders of the Germans, who sent them to the most dangerous places, especially to fight partisans in the forests.

Before the operation in July 1944, the leader of the Kalmucks, Boris Naminzov, handed over all of their rubles to Jan Pamuła. They didn't need them anymore, they were preparing themselves for death, were ready for it! They were aware of what the Soviets would do to them; they wouldn't go to a POW camp, they would rather die.

They left behind a calling-card -- one of the raped women from Rzeczyca Okrągła got pregnant. She wanted an abortion, she had children, a husband, but he refused his permission -- it's God's innocent creature, let the three of us live together. A boy was born with a flat face, slanted eyes, swarthy skin, raven black eyes, who lived here until recently.

* * *

Mr. Antoni Madurski (1929), retired Polish Army colonel from Warsaw, native of Dąbrowa Rzeczyca, always admired "old man" Kosiński. For the gauntlet thrown down to the Germans. For wisdom and courage, thanks to which he saved not only himself and his family but also little Henio.

He didn't go to the ghetto and concentration camp like the rest of his countrymen. He didn't stay behind a wardrobe or in a cellar, waiting for someone to give him a piece of bread, to take out the pail. Despite his rather bad "appearance,"

disastrous in the case of his wife and son, he spent two and a half years with his family in conditions that were exceptional, in spite of everything.

To be sure, in fear of being turned in, in fear of the Germans, of the partisans, of bandits pretending to be partisans; remaining on his guard, but not even hiding, living almost normally! Certainly in limited freedom, but in freedom none the less. He worked, gave lessons, went to neighboring villages for food, talked politics, even dropped in on peasants' meetings!

Of course, Mrs. Kosiński and the "little one," with the "worse" appearance, stayed in the enclosure, but not behind a wardrobe or in a dug-out! They also went to church, visited neighbors in the barrack. They lived -- taking wartime conditions into account -- in peaches and cream, enjoying the respect of the village.

They surely had luck, money, but so many Jews richer than they perished. So that -- at least in Madurski's opinion -- apart from the attitude of the village, of course, what was more important was the wisdom of the professor, who simply managed to create an almost ideal existence for his family.

How? In what way? For what price? -- that is his secret.

* * *

Though most of the locals believe he must have "paid off" the military police in Zaklików, that's all. It's very likely that he "greased their palms" well, for otherwise how could he have dared to live so openly? To emerge untouched from all encounters with the Germans? There are no miracles. He must have had some guarantee.

Be that as it may, he wanted to survive, he was saddled with two women and two children. The question is, how did he arrange this? Through whom? Poles also worked "at Zaklików," and the Germans, especially after Stalingrad, were already very corrupt and -- here at least -- took care of almost everything "for money." The Germans also differed considerably; some were more conscientious, others less so, and still others were completely derelict in their duties.

And maybe the locals are being unfair to him, but they also wondered whether he wasn't paying for his security by passing along information the Germans needed. Maybe that's why they protected and tolerated him? Maybe that's why they let him live?

The more so as the professor showed up literally everywhere -- in the state purchasing center, in church, at meetings, at the village administrator's house and at the tailor's. The Germans must have had informers -- otherwise would so many partisans and "commies" have gotten caught and even some peasants just for slaughtering swine?

And Kosiński really had the peasants where he wanted them, not only because he was their customer. They often came to see Warchoł, who used to buy pigs from breeders; he was always doing business with them.

For instance, Michal Tryka (1911) of Wola Rzeczycka, who did a bit of "shoe-making," remembers one time when "Kusiński" dropped in and brought some shoes to be repaired. And on this occasion the professor complained that he was weak, had no strength, for he wasn't eating any meat! If each day he could only get a teeny-weeny bit, like a bird's head, he would feel better! And he asked Tryka if by chance he didn't know of any neighbor who was slaughtering swine and selling pork. He would buy a few kilos, would "regain his strength!" Tryka knew, of course, but he wasn't about to babble -- not long ago a woman neighbor from Wola had slaughtered a pig not for sale but for a funeral banquet in honor of her father; someone "sang," and she was sent to Majdanek concentration camp.

This, of course, is no proof; he really may have been looking for a seller. But he provoked questions and suspicions, if only because another Jew was also hiding in Dąbrowa, but in what different circumstances! Karol Liebeskind was younger than the professor, to be sure, less experienced and less affluent, but despite this people their so very different lots.

After all, Karol was from these parts – he knew everything and everybody here. The entire village liked him, helped him as much it could. But he had to die in such a stupid way, unnecessarily, and before this had to suffer for a few years, hiding like a hunted animal, terrified, infested with lice, in dug-outs, hay-stacks. He started to drink moonshine, but could he have endured his humiliation and fear otherwise?

"Kusiński," meanwhile, even though with a "better" appearance than Karol's but with a wife and son of the "worst" appearance, who, when he first came here, knew nobody, never even bothered to hide out. He lived like a vicar, like a king, Mrs. Kosiński, on the other hand, lived like a queen -- except that she had only servants to boss around.

Oh, irony of ironies -- all of this took place in the Liebeskinds' flat! The Kosińskis slept on their beds, ate at their table, used their kitchen utensils. Jurek one day on the porch even leafed through Karol's university course registration book that had been found in a corner.

So is it any wonder that people began to look at "Kusiński's" courage and resourcefulness ever more suspiciously? Even with fear? Though, in Mr. Andrzej Migdałek's opinion, quite unnecessarily, for the Kosińskis feared the Germans. He remembers that well.

The Kosińskis did, indeed, emerge unscathed from encounters with Germans, but only because the local Germans -- "our" Germans, as they were called -- who were stationed in Kępa, guarded the bridge over the river San and weren't particularly interested in the village. Maybe they were afraid, or maybe they just didn't want any trouble. In any case, they were hardly very zealous; they didn't nosy around in the farmsteads, didn't ask questions. As a rule, they limited their contacts with the local population to village administrator Stępak, who knew a little German.

On the other hand, the Gestapo, who were stationed in nearby Zaklików, were no laughing matter. Fortunately, they very rarely came here; and even when they did, the village immediately warned the Kosińskis, for this was in the interest of its residents.

* * *

Mr. Jan Pamuła, the professor's former pupil, is not surprised that the professor worked in the state purchasing center, the local eye of the hurricane. He surely risked a lot -- the military police was always being changed, at any moment he could have been "bumped off" by someone who had not been bought or informed. But it was here that the professor probably arranged for the existence of his family -- was able to be in contact with the entire local community, with the peasants, the partisans, the Germans. He entered into all sorts arrangements, did business. He listened to the latest rumors and news, leaks about impending operations, man-hunts.

Of course, he has his own opinion about the professor, but he also sees the tragic dimensions of this figure. Those of a typical wandering Jew -- constantly fighting for existence and survival, capable of coping in the most difficult circumstances. The long centuries of the diaspora have taught this nation a lot, and old man Kosiński is one of the best examples of this.

Even today Pamuła clearly sees him before his eyes. Short, stooped, hiding his face behind a high collar. Setting out every day not only for food but also for news, contacts, for it was they and not the "wardrobe" that enabled him to survive.

CHAPTER 8

The Commies

Not only Dąbrowa but also the neighboring villages -- Kępa, Wola, Rzeczyca Długa and Okrągła -- had leftist and even communistic tendencies before the war. Mainly out of the poverty that drove people to the local saw-mills, to the steel mill in Stalowa Wola, to which the peasants every day trekked fifteen kilometers in one direction; and it was here that they came into contact with agitators from the East, who promised land, equality and justice.

So on the first of May, the festive procession used to be held in Wola, perhaps the most working-class village; people marched with red banners, sang the *International, To the Barricades.* In the saw-mill in Kępa there was always a strike, until the business finally went bankrupt.

There were a few members of the Polish Communist Party, headed by Franciszek Delbas, radical members of the Peasants' Party, members of the Polish Socialist Party, among them Andrzej Warchoł, who got kicked out of the saw-mill in Kępa for trying to unionize the place.

Hence, most active here during the occupation were the leftist, peasant partisans, under the cover of the Food Producers' Cooperative -- the "hammer boys" from the "Hammer and Sickle," but it wasn't long before their leader Delbas was arrested (he subsequently perished in the Majdanek concentration camp). Somewhere around the spring of 1942, after visits by some city "slickers," all the way from Warsaw, people say, the "Delbas boys," as people sometimes called the "Reds," became ever more active, started making the rounds, and once again supposedly established some organization, which later turned out to be -- the Polish Workers' Party.

The founders were the most important members, in Wola for example it was Michał and Ludwik Pawelec, Delbaska (Delbas' widow), Michał Stelbach, Roman Wojtala; in Rzeczyca Okrągła -- Roman Turek; in Dąbrowa -- Kazimierz Tracz, Franciszek Jóźwiak.

All of them, one must admit, were ideological pre-war communists, smart, brighter than most of the local peasants.

But despite all their persuasion and promises of "golden mountains", all they got were the worst of the lot. The illiterate, old and uneducated, that is the stupid and the dangerous.

Among the recruits was Antoni B. who once wanted to shoot his own uncle because he didn't like his views. He was stopped literally at the last moment. Andrzej Ch., who, just after the war, during a speech at a rally in place of "we patriots," said "we idiots." Then he wondered why people were falling over with laughter. Michał R., who forcibly turned back women carrying butter and milk to the village market, because it was "for the masters."

The rest of them belonged to a group, that even before the war, entered the church in Wola and tried to hang the red banner over the altar. This caused a scuffle with Pastor Sebastiański who would not allow such profanation. He later brought in the best missionaries to preach on the subject of the "Bolshevik disease." But he did not get good results. The church in Wola was never full to capacity, not even during the Holy Days, like the churches in the other villages, though it is quite probable that poverty was part of the cause. It was expected that one dress well for church, have shoes, and drop 5 groszy on the collection plate.

These PWP members were called "commies" or "duraks" and were laughed at, for the Red Army was still far away and here they were getting themselves warmed up for a better life and easy bread! But what can one say, people are people, and they will line up according to which way the wind blows.

To keep under cover, they did not hold open meetings; when they had to meet, they took to the forest. They "conspired" in small groups. For example, those from Dąbrowa, at Kazimierz T.'s house, the most important of the "commies."

One day, however, Andrzej Warchoł was astonished to see them coming out his barrack, to be precise out of the Kosińskis' flat!

He thought this was an accident, but when he saw them a second time, he lost his temper and sent them packing. He was the landlord, it was his right. This was his yard, his barrack and -- in a certain sense -- also "his" Jew, for whom he was risking his neck, and so he thought he was entitled to know who came calling, who was tempting the fates!

They retorted just as angrily, threatened that someday they would get even with those who were not with them! This didn't surprise him at all -- since a long time they had a bone to pick with him. They had asked him to join the PWP, merge his PSP organization with theirs. He refused, however, and probably in no uncertain terms. For, though he had leftist tendencies, he was no communist! He was a Polish socialist and not a "commie"! His PSP was made up of the rural aristocracy and not down-and-outs like the PWP!

He didn't even want to talk with them. To renounce God? Promote collective farms, maybe even common wives? Have headquarters in Moscow and take orders from there? Not in your life!

✳ ✳ ✳

When plied with questions about his new "cronies," Kosiński equivocated, saying that he played chess with one of them, while the others watched -- that's all.

And, in fact, it supposedly did start from games of chess with Kołodziej of Wola, who was a strong player; though he was a peasant, he belonged to the village aristocracy -- from the richest family here for generations. Besides this, an educated, religious family; old man Kołodziej had bought the land for construction of the church in Wola. Only his son Stach had gone astray, had gotten tied up with the "Reds," and during games of chess tried to get Kosiński to join them.

Soon, however, Kosiński stopped equivocating, for though the "Reds" had pseudonyms, were supposedly acting under cover, it was hard to keep things "hush- hush" in the village; and so it wasn't long before everyone knew that he was "hobnobbing" with "commies," "blockheads." He had become a "Bolshie"!

$*$ $*$ $*$

As Edward and Antoni Madurski tell it, Franciszek Jóźwiak persuaded their father, Józef of Dąbrowa Rzeczycka, to join the PWP. For Jóźwiak came from the same village as Madurski's wife, and -- like the Madurski boys -- had been in the prewar Polish police force. He promised wonders -- land, free schools for his sons, so Józef Madurski was won over and even attended a meeting. One of those present was Kosiński, who on the way home successfully talked him out of belonging to the PWP.

"This isn't a party for Madurski!" -- he explained. – "You are a decent, quiet man, a practicing Catholic! A former policeman, that also means something! There, on the other hand - it can't be concealed, everyone knows what a bunch of jerks they are! With me it's a different story! I'm the brains of the party!"

And he wasn't stretching the truth -- he really was the biggest brain, the egghead and double-dome of the entire locality.

So people wondered why he had"tied-up" with them. A supposedly wise and educated person -- together with "illiterates," "numskulls" dreaming of collective farms and revolution? Reaching out their grubby hands for other people's property -- the estates of the Lubomirskis, the Tamowskis, the Dolańskis?

Had he suddenly become converted to their "religion," since before this, in conversations about the military situation, he had always emphasized that he was very familiar with it and said he knew what a danger it posed to Poland? He said that he had been in Russia during the revolution; in any case, he was very fluent in Russian.

So no one doubted that he had become "palsy-walsy" with them for the sake of his own religion, that is, for his survival. The war was still going on, and he wanted to live, wanted to save his family, and so he looked for support even from "numskulls," but who had their own underground army.

And "numskulls" with a future, as he was already becoming aware. So, even though everyone poked fun at them, he ignored this completely and remained with them to the end -- until his departure, or rather flight, in April 1945.

Or had he perhaps gone over to them out of fear? After all, he was a so- called *pomyeshchik,* that is, a property owner, a rich manufacturer, a "bloodsucker" and "enemy of the people." Did he want to protect himself? Take out insurance? Come to an understanding with the new authorities?

* * *

Most of the Polish Workers' Party men of those days lie in their graves, with a few exceptions. One of them is Mr. Ludwik Pawelec (1925) of Wola Rzeczycka, who today lives in Warsaw and probably made the most successful career of anyone from these parts, for he served in the diplomatic corps.

Who's Who in Poland of 1984 informs that in 1946-1961 he was a government employee, since 1961 -- in the diplomatic corps; Polish consul general in Sweden, member of PWP -- 1942-1948; PUWP -- since 1948, decorated with the Silver and Bronze Cross of Merit, among other distinctions.

Of course, he remembers Mieczysław Kosiński, but has forgotten his pseudonym as a member of the PWP cell in Dąbrowa Rzeczycka.

And he remembers him as an active, conspicuous member, though not like such organizers as Mr. Pawelec's brother Michał, lgnacy Moskal, Michał Stelmach, or those from the forest cells -- the famous Paleniów brothers, Andrzej, pseudonym "Eagle" and Jan, "Falcon," leaders of the People's Guard and subsequently of the People's Army.

Kosiński was recruited by his brother Michał, who acted on orders from the central cell in neighboring Skowierzyna, which had been observing the professor since a long time. A professor from Łódź, with leftist views - maybe he could be useful to the party? So they instructed Michal Stelmach to check him out -who was he, really? Where was he from? They supposedly even sent someone to Łódź, where they had a contact; they sent their own man, for they didn't want to reply on anyone they couldn't trust.

The investigation was favorable, and Kosiński himself was eager to cooperate -- smart, savvy in politics, understanding that they were the heavyweights here and would soon be in the saddle. So he was sworn in and pledged allegiance to the party, was assigned to the cell in Dąbrowa, where he lived; the main cell was in Wola.

He was surely taking a risk, but was it really so great? He was one of many members, known to few, not from here. It was the brother of Ludwik Pawelec and Delbas's wife who were assigned the major leadership roles -- and they paid for this with their lives.

To stay under cover they most often only contacted the cell secretaries, met in threes, fives, and in a larger group only for an operation. It even happened that not all of the colleagues (they started to call each other "comrade" only after the Russians arrived) knew of each other, until a certain time.

Mr. Ludwik Pawelec, however, had contacts with every one of them – he distributed leaflets and the press, *Gwardzista* and *Trybuna Wolności,* which he picked up in Janiki, concealed under his jacket, under the seat of his bike, and delivered to Kosiński, among others. He used to show up at Kosiński's place around three or four in the morning, when everyone else was sleeping; no one saw them. Before partisan operations he also used to drop off weapons to Kosiński, who was supposed to pass them along -- like the press.

For them he was also the "professor" -- he taught, gave additional instruction,

but mainly to those who had predispositions for moving up the career ladder. He held special classes for them -- for peasants who had completed only a few years of elementary school, who also had gained some experience in prisons and under arrest. He confined himself to explaining the basic concepts -- Marxism, the class struggle, internationalism.

A few of them, however, including some from the forest cells, were elementary school graduates, and so he prepared them for the secondary-school certificate. And he must have done a pretty good job, for they later passed without any problems in Lublin. Mr. Pawelec was also slated to be one of his pupils, but he got caught up in his agitation activities and postponed his secondary school graduation.

What is most important - - Kosiński helped them a lot in work on the agricultural reform that they planned to carry out right after the Germans left and just before the Russians entered, but they didn't manage. He drew up an excellent plan for the division of the landed estate in Charzewica, which, among other villages, was composed of Dąbrowa, Kępa, Rzeczyca Długa and Okrągła. Though he wasn't from here, they supplied him with materials, access to the p r o p e r t y , which they sliced up after the war according to his plans, and so in a sense this is a monument to him.

They knew, of course, about his origins and his situation, and that is why they extended such an impermeable umbrella over him. They even had instructions from the party to say -- if it were at all possible -- that he is a Pole, that his house in Łódź had burned down, and he had come here, to his relatives, etc.

Mr. Pawalec also recalls when he was in Wola one day and one of his colleagues instructed him to "hotfoot it" to Dąbrowa to warn the professor, for the Germans were coming!

So Kosiński survived thanks to the PWP, which protected and screened him; even though the lads were decent sorts, there might have been a bad apple among them -- but would anyone have had the guts to "rat" on a fellow member?

They mainly protected him against the Germans, who only ventured here on military operations; otherwise they looked in here rarely -- they were afraid of the partisans; the People's Guard and then the People's Army had their headquarters here.

Thus, not only Dąbrowa saved the Kosińskis but also the party and its underground army. In short, their saviors were the PWP, PG, PA.

For his son, for Jerzy Kosiński, this unquestionably wasn't the most pleasant truth, but it was the unvarnished truth.

* * *

Soon after the war they scattered, went their separate ways -- to the army, to the police, to the security force. Marysia Korga from the Skowierzyna organization became the first secretary of the party in Tarnobrzeg, and she naturally brought in her own people.

Mr. Ludwik Pawelec without hesitation - already in August 1994 – entered the army and doesn't even know what happened to comrade Kosiński after that. Where did he end up? Did he get some assignment?

For, very oddly, after this the professor never sent any news, didn't write a word, even though the local Polish Workers' Party boys have held reunions, meetings -- to this day the dwindling band keeps in touch with one another.

Pawalec is soon expecting another visit by Marek from Denmark, in truth Motełe lmmergluck, a Jew from Radomyśl, a Polish Workers' Party member from Wola -- but only from 1944; during the occupation he had to flee to the Soviet Union. They will reminisce, enumerate who has had a heart attack, who has died, but above all they will sing, for Motełe is a fine singer, who once used to sing in Wola at the first of May celebrations, but who today sings in the Copenhagen synagogue.

Kosiński, on the other hand, even though he spent a "blue moon" with them, never even sent them a word of greeting, and so they felt resentment against him, as they later did against his son.

* * *

"As long as the night of the occupation lasted" -- Edward Warchoł recalls -- "there were no problems with the Kosińskis, and no one thought there ever would be any." But as time passed, he became ever less sure of this, especially after the "thunder" started to be heard from the East and after Kosiński had turned "Bolshie."

Kosiński even got so "cocky" that he stopped paying Warchoł rent. At first, he promised that he would pay tomorrow, the day after tomorrow, until he finally made no bones that he wouldn't pay at all. From what? He was completely "busted"!

The professor also more and more often started to return from the "commies" plastered" especially after the drops of Soviet "parachutists" -- who later turned out to be NKVD agents. On one occasion, when he apparently was too lazy to go into the forest to gather dry twigs, he chopped up part of the fence encircling the barrack for firewood! A few days later he wanted to do this again, but this time Warchoł sensed what he was up to, rushed out of the barrack, called him everything under the sun. How dared he destroy someone else's property?

Kosiński, on the other hand, instead of keeping silent as before, started to shout ever more loudly. That this fence wasn't Warchoł's at all! The Soviets were approaching and -- who knows? -- maybe everything will be common property? So why all of this fuss?

In fact, Kosiński "grew fangs" -- at that time he also picked a fight with the Migdałeks, his neighbors in the barrack. And it was over buttermilk.

The Migdałeks were now faring better. Mrs. Migdałek had started to trade in cloth and tobacco. She used to go to Rzeszów for goods, which she then sold in Dąbrowa and the vicinity. So they started to buy more food, could afford a few luxuries -- milk and butter, which were delivered by a peasant woman from Kępa, who left them on the doorstep when they weren't home. But when they returned one day, only the milk was there. They asked neighbors what had happened to the buttermilk, which Mr. Migdałek liked to drink, and it turned out that professor Kosiński had taken it!

Mr. Migdałek immediately went over to the professor's to complain -- how could he? Really a trifle, but someone else's! Kosiński, however, said it was his right, that it was coming to him! There has to be justice -- if one person has butter, the other must have buttermilk! Jurek and Henio are also crazy about it!

"That's the way communists think." -- retorted Mr. Migdałek and never spoke with the professor again.

The same experience befell Mr. Zbigniew Feliks Bączkowski, captain of the Home Army, who later fell in the Warsaw Uprising, and who used to come to Dąbrowa to visit his wife and children, whom he had brought here from Warsaw to wait out the occupation.

"Kosiński" -- Bączkowski junior recalls – "made no secret of his sympathies. Why all of these actions of the Home Army? The Uprising? Whom are we defending ourselves against and what for? We are definitely fated to live under Soviet domination! We have to reconcile ourselves to this, we have to decide if we want to live or not."

Mr. Jan Pamuła in turn remembers how the professor sometimes used to query him at lessons about his views. But that's not surprising -- Jan's father was in the Home Army, he himself had barely escaped being deported for forced labor, and his mother was very religious, of which the thirteen-year-old made no secret; and so the professor worried, warned him that in the Poland which would arise he would have nothing but troubles. However, fortunately he was young, and there was still time to change his way of thinking.

It was no secret what the punishment was for hiding Kosiński, but he meanwhile -- though he had money for a maid, for meat -- didn't pay his rent, chopped down the fence, "tied-up with the commies." Warchoł, who was the landlord and was associated with the Home Army, long since could have sent him packing, could simply have given him notice. Could have put his things out on the street, as would have happened to all tenants who didn't pay their rent!

But he was afraid, for notwithstanding the death penalty he traded in pork. He made the rounds of the villages and bought meat from pig-breeders. So he was afraid that Kosiński would "squeal" on him "to Zaklików," with which -- people whispered -- he was in "cahoots," for how otherwise would he have dared to show his face everywhere so openly? For what would have happened if a Polish blue policeman or a gendarme had dropped into the barrack and spotted Jurek and Mrs. Kosiński?!

What is more, Kosiński soon established contacts with the Red partisans, and not ordinary partisans, not with ones he could complain about. With Roman Jóźwiak, the son of neighbors, platoon leader, not stupid, educated -- having completed a few years of grammar-school -- but who was later killed in the forest. With Roman Rybak, partisan of various shades, first White, then Red, executed in 1945 by the National Guard. They dropped in often, usually in the evening, supposedly for German lessons. They always came with the Red press, leaflets, which they then lent to Warchoł, when things were still okay between him and Kosiński. And he in return repaid him with the Home Army *Wolność i Szczerbiec,* which he distributed.

But later there was nothing to talk about -- Kosiński threw in his lot with the "Bolshies," who had not only friends but entire units in the forest. The partisans didn't mollycoddle anybody; they settled their scores at night. Those were times when human life was worth nothing -- entire villages were burned down, people's brains were blown out in broad daylight. Power was in the hands of those who had weapons and could get away with taking revenge against their enemies, whom it was better not to have and to lie low. During the day the Germans used to come by, at night the partisans -- first Whites, then Reds, and after them thugs who literally stole the shirts off people's backs.

So, could he throw Kosiński out? The more so as he had already gotten one lesson from the partisans and didn't want another one.

Today it is hard to say just when this happened; in any case, Warchoł was awakened one night by a terrible racket. An armed band broke down the door with their rifle butts, dragged him out of the house to the marsh, where they beat him until he lost consciousness. He begged for mercy -- said he had a wife, children, farm. However, the young men escorting him said that it wasn't up to them - it was for the commander to decide! So Warchoł begged him for mercy, but, unmoved, in Russian the commander gave the order to shoot. Miraculously, the bullet only gazed Warchoł, but he fell and pretended to be dead. They grabbed him by the arms and dragged him through the mud toward a nearby pond, where -- as they discussed among themselves -- they wanted to throw him in. But he was heavy, so they left him there in the bog. After they were gone, he tried to get up but couldn't, so he crawled to a nearby house, where people dressed his wound, washed the blood off him.

For a long time after this, he didn't sleep in his own house. Mr. Andrzej Migdałek remembers how Warchoł used to come to his house at night; he sat at the table, held his face in his hands and dozed until dawn. In time, he recovered. The Migdałeks eventually had to flee from Dąbrowa to escape from the partisans.

Warchoł never did find out who had wanted to blow his brains out -- or just scare him. It surely wasn't the bandits, for they didn't know anything. Clearly, it was the Red partisans -- for theirs were the only units that had Russians, most of whom were either parachutists or escaped POWs. People say that the unit responsible was headed by Palenie, pseudonym "Eagle," of Lipa, commander of the People's Guard and then of People's Army units. But what was their reason? Was it for Warchoł's contacts with the Home Army? For his Polish Socialist Party past? For refusing to cooperate with the "commies"?

All this is possible, but it is no secret whom he suspected. For who had contacts with them? Who had a reason to frighten him? To prevent him from throwing him out? To show what he could do?

And he did indeed show what he was capable of, and so Warchoł started to fear Kosiński. He now feared the man whom he had sheltered. What would happen if Kosiński complained about him again? It might be much worse for him this time.

And so he put up his non-paying guest, waiting for the fortunately imminent end of the occupation. Just a little while longer and Kosiński would finally be gone!

Yet, people are only people, and soon they had another confrontation. This time it was over wood, since fuel was one of the basic necessities. In the spring of 1944 Warchoł got permission to chop down and buy wood from the forest but had no means of transportation. Kosiński, however, who had learned of this from tenants in the barrack, delivered the wood and also arranged for customers. But Warchoł had no intention of selling; that was his business and he would decide! He didn't want to have any dealings withKosiński!

Of course, he told him all of this in no uncertain terms, and to make matters worse was a little tipsy, and so was Kosiński! Both of them shouted and cursed each other, using the familiar form ofaddress.

Warchoł finally chased him away, ordered him to move out at once, and as if out of spite -- started insulting him by calling him a Kike. Kosiński in tum called Warchoł a boor and shouted that he would still show him, would give Warchoł something to remember him by!

On the next day, after both of them had calmed down and sobered up, Kosiński had no intention of moving out or Warchoł of throwing him out. He just stopped talking to him, steered clear of him completely -- he was afraid of him. He consoled himself with the thought that the troubles were ending -- the Germans had started to run away, the sounds of the approaching front could be heard, the Red Army was coming.

* * *

The Red Army entered Dąbrowa on 28 July, 1944, right after the harvest. Most of the village, driving their cows and goats before them, had run off to the forest earlier -- for who knew what might happen? The only people left were "commies" with their families, among them the Kosińskis, even though the rest of the barrack had cleared out. They greeted the Red Army boys with flowers, speeches, red flags with the hammer and sickle. The most enthusiastic welcome came from professor "Kusiński," who was drunk with joy, happy as never before!

From the very start he gained their affection -- he greeted them together with Henio, whom he had dressed in an earlier prepared Red Anny uniform -- in a soldier's blouse, a red shirt with a stand-up collar, girded with a soldier's belt, green trousers, a field-cap with a red star. With a string to his belt he attached an automatic pistol carved from wood, with which the boy refused to part; he aimed and shouted: "Hurrah, hurrah, fighters!" People thought that this was just for the welcoming, but no -- Henio wore the uniform all the time, which obviously delighted the Red Army men, who took him up in their arms, hugged and kissed him! He became their mascot, the son of the regiment.

They didn't kill, they didn't bum. So the people of Dąbrowa slowly came out of the forest and returned to their homes. And to tell the truth, they also greeted the Soviets with joy, for they were liberators, victors, the war was finally over! And no one, as was related in *The Painted Bird,* killed them, there was no "incident." On the contrary, people showed them kindness, which they returned. They treated the children with candy, the adults with vodka, and in Rzeczyca Okrągła they opened up a field hospital, where their doctor also treated the local population. In Dąbrowa, however, close to the barracks in which the Kosińskis lived, they dug anti-tank pits, which they covered with branches.

Of course, they requisitioned most of the better cottages for billets, but their needs were simple -- some hay strewn on the floor for sleeping, some rags on which several of them lay down together. In one of the empty flats they set up a field kitchen; they cooked soup from drawn fowl, treated children from the barracks --

Stefcia and Edzio as well as Jurek and Henio Kosiński, Zbyszek Bączkowski. They took photos of the children, for one of the soldiers had a camera. Mr. Zbigniew Bączkowski even kept them for many years, but finally destroyed them. Who knew that someday they would be important?

The flats were occupied by the officers -- platoon leaders, majors, high-ranking NKVD men, who had come along with the army. Where the front is, there we are, they said. At Warchoł's -- an NKVD man with several bars, with guards watching over him day and night. At the Kosińskis' -- two majors. At Mrs. Bączkowski's - also some important officer, for he had an orderly.

This officer stayed under her roof only a few days, however, for she moved heaven and earth and quickly got him evicted. She went literally everywhere -- to

77

Warchoł, for there was no landlord, to the village administrator, and to probably all of the senior officers. She shouted, sobbed -- she is young, alone, just with her children, so how does it look for a man to be living and sleeping under her roof? She didn't say, of course, that she simply didn't want him there. After all, her husband was fighting in the Warsaw Uprising, while a Soviet officer was living in her flat!

And she somehow got rid of him; he finally went elsewhere, and during the several days in which he lived in her place she did everything she could to keep him at arm's length. She behaved like a typical proud Polish woman: she spoke with him only as much as she had to; he slept with his orderly in the kitchen, where he also took his meals; she couldn't bear to watch him eating a chicken and -- throwing the bones to his orderly!

And it's no secret that she looked at the Kosińskis with loathing, for they had become thick as thieves with their roomers. They talked, ate, and took walks with them. And in the evenings, they fixed grand suppers for them with ample booze; the merrymaking could be heard throughout the barrack, for they sang *Katyusha*. They turned Henio into their plaything, the laughing-stock of the village.

Mrs. Bogumita Jóźwiak of Dąbrowa, nicknamed Bośka, recalls one scene · connected with this. With the rest of the village of Dąbrowa she happened to be working on the bridge over the river San, which the Germans had blown up and the Russians were now rebuilding. The Russians were supervising the work, riding around in their "Zils" and in one with an open cab they were transporting Henio – the little Red Army lad in uniform, whom they gloried in, praised, passed from hand to hand.

Dąbrowa on the other hand didn't have much good to say about this. Why hadn't they made Jurek the son of the regiment instead of Henio, who was an orphan and still understood little? When his new "friends" weren't around, the boys threw stones at him and shouted: "Commie, with farts in your pants!"

Jurek, on the other hand, hung on the fence as usual, didn't stick his nose out of the compound, while the "old man" paraded around everywhere only with Henio.

To be exact, nearly everywhere, for the professor, of course, went alone to the evening drinking bouts at the forester's lodge. It was there that the Red Anny men had set up their command headquarters. There they had more room, freedom, were not so conspicuous. The Forester Liber had to host them -- he worked in the forest, the most sensitive point here; he had already gotten used to the fact that he had to get along with everybody -- with partisans of all shades, with the Germans, and then with the Soviets. Anyway, he was no teetotaler, and the Soviets were real heavy drinkers; they even added carbide to moonshine to "give it strength." On the occasion of the anniversary of the October Revolution they drank for a few days. *"Tovaryshch profyesor,"* as they called Kosiński, was their frequent guest in the forester's lodge, as were most of the "commies," who worked closely with the Red Army men.

He -- as well as the other "Bolshies" -- also used to visit the main headquarters in Jastkowice, right by Zaklików, command center of the NKVD men, whom the Red Army soldiers themselves feared, since for the slightest infraction one could be sent by them to the *karnoy roty* -- to a penal company, to the front line!

Besides, the Red Army boys, even the high-ranking ones, were simple peasants, the NKVD men on the other hand -- intelligent, educated, shrewd. They made the rounds of the houses to chat, to help, but really -- to gather information about this or that. One of them was Alek Sashka, who used to go around with the professor. They say that Alek was a university graduate and had a first-rate mind.

Stanisław Temporale (1926) of Dąbrowa Rzeczyca was then a young man. Despite the order of the Soviets to hand over weapons immediately, he concealed a pistol in a hay-stack. Just out of stupidity. He got a thrill out of having a "gat" with which he could impress his girl. But apparently someone suspected and "stooled" on him, for the NKVD came, found the weapon, and took Temporale to Jastkowice.

He thought that his number was up -- for the illegal possession of a weapon they could have deported him to Siberia or had him shot in the Głogów forest. And without any legal niceties -- justice was handed down by military courts. But when the officer conducting the interrogation learned that Temporale was from Dąbrowa, he immediately sent for *tovaryshch profyesor.* When the latter arrived, they greeted him warmly -- *zdrastvuytye, zdrastvuytye!* They asked about Temporale, and the professor was quick to say that he was a reliable sort, not mixed up in politics of any kind, which was the truth. "I vouch for him completely!" -- Kosiński said. His opinion apparently carried a lot of weight with them, for Temporale was soon released and to this day is one of "Kusiński's" biggest fans; thankful, he praises him to the skies. "A great guy!" - he says to everybody. "It's only thanks to him that the NKVD let me go!"

At that time Kosiński was quite active, as were all of the "Reds," who wasted no time in setting up the "people[1]s government" in collaboration with the Soviets. Mr. Antoni Madurski, also a native of Dąbrowa, recalls that in September or October of 1944, in any case, soon after the Russians had arrived, he used to take Kosiński regularly in his cart to Tarnobrzeg, the district capital. He waited for him in front of the newly forming offices -- the district people's council, the police, where Kosiński had business. But what kind of business Madurski obviously didn't dare to ask, for at that time he was only Toni of Dąbrowa, who drove and waited, that's all.

He also remembers the professor translating impromptu, for he was very fluent in Russian, the proclamations and announcements pasted by the Soviets on posts. People also say that, in cooperation with the Soviets, he had arranged for the arrival of Wanda Wasilewska herself,* whose presence was supposed to crown the official opening of the bridge over the river San. But she didn't show up, and who can blame her? -- to such a god-forsaken hole? Maybe she feared that on this occasion there would be a Holy Mass and a blessing of the bridge?

Mrs. Migdałek returned to Dąbrowa toward the end of July 1944 to harvest the millet that she had previously sown.

She happened to be walking through the village when she suddenly spotted professor Kosiński with two NKVD men. She had never seen him like

---

* Wanda Wasilewska (1905-64), communist party activist, co-founder of the Union of Polish Patriots and the First Polish Army, both in the Soviet Union.

this before -- ebullient, smiling, speaking loudly and with animation, gesticulating, explaining, while the other two listened.

He didn't greet her, which really was no surprise to her, for this had happened before -- he was very near-sighted. But when she asked the neighbors about him, they said that he no longer recognizes anybody. He only hobnobs with the "upper crust" -- with the NKVD men, with senior officers. He really thinks he is somebody, and it's better to watch out for him -- who knows what he's telling them?

CHAPTER 9

Shades of Judas

Sometime around the beginning of October 1944, the NKVD men who were billeted at Warchoł's suddenly said to him, right out of the blue:

"Khazyain, tebya nada idti na rabotu!"*

"Where?" -- Warchoł asked in surprise – "and what for?"

"Gdye, ni znayu" – the former explained – *"no ukhodi i na do/go! Patom vyernyoshshya, no tyepyer ukhodi!"***

This was furthest from Warchoł's mind -- as usual he had his hands full of work, so how could he *ukhodit'?* And why?

So he ignored the warning, even laughed at it, for thank the Lord, the Germans had long since departed and the war was over!

To be sure, like many of his neighbors, he had been a member of the Home Army, but only a private. He hadn't hid out in the forest but had been only a sympathizer: he had fed them, led them through the forest, distributed newspapers.

Yet, people started to whisper that the "Russkies" were arresting people, sending them to Siberia, but everyone thought that this concerned only the "top echelons" of the Home Army -- the officers, leaders of partisan units, district commanders. Why would they be interested in simple peasants who should be tilling the fields?

---

* Landlord, you should go to work!

** Where, I don't know, but you should go away and for a long time! Later you may come back, but now go away!

* * *

Several days later he was awakened out of a sound sleep by a banging at the door, a real hullabaloo, shouts. He opened the door, and NKVD men rushed in with automatic pistols, ordered him to *sabiratsya!**They stripped the ring and watch from his hand! One of them took a piece of paper out of his pocket and read some "accusation," charging Warchoł of collaboration with the Germans, of being a member of the farm levies commission, which was a fact, and of having a "hostile attitude to the party and the Red Army."

The accusation had been signed by two local "Reds," which the Soviets were quick to emphasize. *"Zhalko nam tyebye"* -- they said – *"no eto nye nashe dyelo, tolko vashych ludyey!"***

They, of course, knew no one here, knew nothing about anyone, for, how should they? They were only carrying out the justice of the people! They were removing the enemies of the people!

He wanted to explain that if he had collaborated with the Germans, he wouldn't have concealed a Jew, but they quickly pushed him into the Black Maria parked in front of the house, in which several neighbors from Dąbrowa and the vicinity were already sitting.

* * *

In fact, most of those connected with the Home Army who had ever had any "run-ins" with the "commies," such as Adam Szkutinik of Wola, a participant of the war of 1920. In the main, those rounded up were the local cream of the crop -- the most well-off, the most intelligent, the most active. Everyone who mattered, such as village administrator Józef Stępak of Kępa, Władysław Pamuła of Wola, Jan Surma of Rzeczyca Okrągła. And also Wojciech Świątek -- one of the richest, Józef Gagata of Dąbrowa -- one of the most intelligent, who knew German and had worked in the Stalowa Wola Steel Mill, where they didn't hire illiterates.

---

* Pack his belongings!

** We're sorry for you, but this isn't our fault but your people's!

Andrzej Rachwalski of Rzeczyca Długa. Most of the members of the farm levies commission, which was made up of the most literate and enterprising persons, including village administrators, ex officio members, and Warchoł, of course.

They were taken to Jastkowice, to field prisons -- pits covered with logs. After a few days -- to the prison in Rzeszów, in November -- in cattle cars to the processing camp in Bokończyce around Przemyśl, and from there -- to Siberia, to the *gulags* around lake Lagoda in Borovitchi and Yegolsk, which most of them, including Stępak, Gugała, Świątek, did not survive. A few returned, among them Szkutnik, Surma.

* * *

Jan Szkutnik of Wola, son of the imprisoned Adam, remembers that night. *"Ty buzhuy, kotoriy zhdyosh polskich panov z Londyna?"* -- he asked father. - "*Ty boroslya z Pilsudskim?"*

And they ran up to the attic and brought down Pilsudski's portrait -- they were well informed! They also read him the "accusation" charging him of belonging to the "so-called Home Army - a fascist organization." The accusation had been signed by two just recently come of age sons of one of the "commies," who a few days earlier had burst into Szkutnik's and started to drag out a heifer, supposedly for the Red Army men. After a bitter quarrel, scuffle, Szkutnik finally let the heifer go -- they had guns, their father was already one of the people's officials, and everyone gave them a wide berth. As they were leaving, he just couldn't keep it in him -- he called them thieves, Bolshies. And, apparently, they got even with him for that, for he was sent to the camp in Borowicze, which he survived and came home in 1947.

* * *

---

[*] You're bourgeois. Are you waiting for your Polish lords from London? Did you fight with Pilsudski?

For Jozef Stępak -- recalls his son Ferdynand – "there came two NKVD men" and Jan P., who lives to this day -- a new "red" village administrator appointed by the Soviets. He was a direct neighbor of Stępak's and had been on the outs with him for a long time. Jan P. put up red flags, while Stępak, who, after all, was the village administrator, took them down. Jan P. read him the "accusation" of "belonging to the Home Army" and "collaboration," that is, being on the "farm levies commission," though as village administrator he was required to serve on the commission. Failure to meet the levies would have resulted in sanctions; he had been locked up several times, and when the delays were too long -- the entire commission was put behind bars.

The accusation was signed by two "commies," probably two of the biggest "boobies," and Jan P., who was a real fanatic, led him away; Stępak's wife and children saw him for the last time, he didn't survive the *gulag,* he probably died from a mental breakdown -- he left a wife and four small children.

* * *

Jan P. (1907), who is ending his days, excuses himself on account of age, but when he wants to -- he remembers.

He admits that at that time he did go around with the NKVD men, but he was already the village administrator, so they ordered him to! But he never turned anyone in, he protected people! Not only "commies" were "stoolies" but ordinary village folk -- Judases! They ran to the Soviets, to headquarters, and complained against their neighbors, against whom they had had a grudge for a long time. Most often against those who watched over the levy of agricultural products and took people's last liter of milk!

Now these people could pay them back, get even -- they took an inch, I'll take a mile -- they gloated! Who knew it would be that bad? Siberia, the *gulag,* death? If they had, maybe they would have buttoned their lips!

* * *

As a result, several random people were also taken away -- poor, illiterate, with no interest in politics, most probably the victims of denunciations. In Kępa one of the "commies" was even arrested; though she was quickly released, she had been scared out of her wits.

* * *

Mrs. Stępak ran after her husband. She wanted to know where they were taking him, but they turned her back, chased her away -- recalls her daughter, Leokadia Nieznalska of Stalowa Wola. She waited a while, then ran to Dąbrowa, to Mrs. Warchoł, whose husband also had been taken away. When it became light, they ran over to Kosiński for help. The wisest man in the village, and what is more important -- the authorities, the *nachalstvo,* respect him. Thanks to him, they released Temporale, maybe he would intercede once more?

But he wasn't at home, and the professor's wife -- pale, scared stiff -- received them in the doorway, explaining that her husband had gone out, that he didn't say when he would be back, and besides -- he has nothing to do with this!

However, they waited until he returned and wept, implored. Only he could help -- he knows whom to go to, who decides! He can write a letter, bring it to the proper person.

He received them coldly, didn't offer a single word of cheer, said that it was surely some mistake and that the boys would soon return home, he was certain of that! They didn't believe him, of course, and didn't want to leave, so he finally promised to find out what it was about and to help if he could.

When they returned in a few days as he had asked, he spread his arms helplessly -- nothing could be done. It was too late, the matter had been decided! And this was true - they had been taken away immediately.

* * *

Yet, Warchoł was rather lucky; he didn't go to Siberia like the others. He was left in the prison in Rzeszów, and people whispered that maybe this was thanks to Kosiński, who vouched for him. Had his conscience bothered him?

However, Warchoł himself -- as his children recollect -- always thought that it was just the opposite. That though the "accusation" had been signed by others, Kosiński also must have had a hand in it. For he was with those who took, and hadn't he threatened him? Hadn't he shouted that Warchoł would remember him? Hadn't he been at odds with him since a long time?

What is more -- during one of the interrogations before the trial he saw his "accusation" written in Kosiński's hand; he was familiar with his handwriting -- they had lived together for such a long time.

Warchoł didn't go to Siberia, into oblivion, for -- as he thought, at least -- he was supposed to be punished immediately, on the spot. Who could have expected that he would encounter honest judges in such terrible times? They listened to the witnesses, who as one man testified that "though he watched over the levy," this was one of the obligations of the village; besides -- he was associated with the Polish Socialist Party, he only distributed the underground press for the Home Army, and, finally, "at the risk of his own life and that of his family's he concealed as a tenant citizen Mieczysław Kosiński of Jewish origin, working for the USSR together with our underground army."

As a result, Warchoł was declared innocent, released; he spent one and a half years in jail waiting for his trial, but what is that in comparison to what befell his neighbors?

* * *

Though the war had supposedly ended, people continued to live "in fear and trembling." And they were even afraid to talk about "that," but talk they did, or rather -- whispered. This was unquestionably the work of the Soviets but carried out so quickly and efficiently thanks to help from local people. "Commies," to be sure, but countrymen none the less. Neighbors, close friends, matchmakers, brothers-in-law, sons-in-laws -- here most people were related by marriage; Kępa, for instance, is one big clan.

But people also whispered about the professor, who, it was alleged, wrote the accusations. The "Bolshies" pressed him to do it -- for who but he could express everything so beautifully? About "reactionary elements"? "Sympathizers of the pro- London underground"? "The so-called Home Army"? None of them could do it, even those with several years of formal schooling!

Besides, he had always been the best in writing; he had also written letters and petitions for village administrator Stępak. He was the person here for writing official letters, the wisest man in the village!

Ferdynand Stępak of Kępa was then fourteen years old; after the deportation of his father he was the oldest man in the family and somehow felt responsible for it. And he remembers that he was completely at a loss as to how he should behave after he heard all of this. Maybe he should somehow "pay back" Kosiński, do something, but what? At least go and ask if this was true.

But he was still just a boy and didn't dare; he was afraid. Moreover, the "old man" was never alone, was always with "them" – "commies," officers -- and after that he quickly fled, "took to his heels."

Ferdynand's mother, however, endured her fate submissively. "In every comer there is misery" -- she said. – "Everywhere there is pain and suffering." And in the end misfortune befell not only her but also so many female neighbors. Yet, in comparison with them she wasn't the worst off, for she still had a rather large piece of land, thanks to which she was somehow able to raise four children. She worked the land together with them, kept body and soul together, remained silent and envied those whose kith and kin had died at the hands of the Germans -- they had their graves, they could speak of them openly, apply for pensions, indemnification.

It wasn't until 1961 that she mustered up the courage to obtain her husband's death certificate, in which she was assisted by her neighbor Surma, who had been with her husband in the *gulag* and wasn't afraid to testify in court that as the camp gravedigger he had personally buried Stępak, that he remembers this well -- he used to cover his countrymen's faces with a newspaper, which was all he could do for them!

* * *

Even though the "Whites" had been decimated by deportations, they weren't napping -- after all, the "Reds" would catch them all like rabbits! Despite the fact that the local Horne Army command was opposed to retaliation, the rank and file, especially the young bucks, were just itching to take action on their own. A new war flared up in earnest, especially a time of settling scores. Especially from the spring of 1945, since before that the Soviet forces were still there, and some units stayed until as late as March.

The "White's" first target were the active members of the Polish Workers' Party. They executed its leading founder -- Michał Pawalec, "Delbaska" -- Delbas's widow, then members of the security force, policemen.

Stefan Tracz of Dąbrowa Rzeczycka, who still lives not far from the old barracks, had an uncle in the Home Army underground, who toward the end of 1944 or beginning of 1945 came to his parents with a secret request.

His unit was supposed to liquidate Kosiński of Dąbrowa -- a "Red," "member of the Polish Workers' Party." The uncle was supposed to lead them to him, and so he asked his cousins for help -- to show where he lived, etc.

"My parents, however, especially my mother'" -- recalls Stefan Tracz – "didn't want to help in the execution of a person, even of someone suspected of the worst. No one had ever caught him red-handed, and besides -- it would be wrong! He had gone through so much, he had survived, and to die after liberation? It would also be a waste of the village's efforts -- it had sheltered him for so many years, exposed itself to danger, and now it was supposed to kill him? Karol Liebeskind had been killed, so let him at least survive! May they leave as quickly as possible, but let's not have Lynch law! Haven't we had enough tragedies?"

The father of Emilia Stec and Jan Pamuła -- Sylwester Pamuła of Rzeczyca Okrągła -- was a member of the Home Army and miraculously escaped being deported. He worked on the railroad and on this occasion was working the night· shift, so they didn't find him at home. He learned of the sentence passed on Kosiński and warned him -- Kosiński taught his son, they visited each others' homes, and in a sense were on friendly terms. So Pamuła thought that he was duty-bound to be loyal to Kosiński. He hadn't yet heard of the suspicions against the professor; they appeared much later.

Father Okoń's friend, Julian Jędrzyjewski, teacher from Radomyśl, an important personage of the local Home Army, would have the most to say about this matter, for he allegedly issued the order, but soon after this he also had to flee.

Likewise, Stanisław Kołodziej of Wola, who had enlisted Kosiński in the PWP. Kołodziej received a warning, got frightened and withdrew from political activities. He moved to the Regained Territories,* to Prudnik -- recalls his sister-in-law, Józef Kołodziej's widow. He soon stopped his communistic activities, for he had become disillusioned right after the arrival of the Russians, who literally on the very first day stripped the gold watch from his wrist.

* * *

On one night toward the end of April 1945 an armed band swept down on the barrack; they broke in the door to the Kosińskis' flat. People heard shouts, a hubbub, the wailing of Henio and Jurek. The intruders did not find Kosiński at home, because he had gone to Łódź, very probably to make arrangements for his departure. No one knows what these men wanted; in any case, they didn't wait around, but took off like a shot.

After it dawned, Mrs. Kosiński rushed out of the house, ran in the direction of the railroad tracks, from where her husband was supposed to return. She waited at the station until noon, when he finally arrived. On the way home, she was seen -- explaining something to him energetically, and then they "powwowed," waving their arms, almost running. She dashed to the barrack, while he went straight to the Krawiecs', who were among the few villagers with a horse; the others had long since gotten rid of their horses (the Germans imposed special levies on their owners -- obligatory transports of wood). Partisans of all sorts also used to sweep down, borrow a horse, and only give it back if and when they pleased.

Krawiec wasn't home, but his son Franciszek was; he still lives in Dąbrowa and remembers everything.

"The 'old man' rushed in like the cops were after him" -- he relates. – "He squeezed some money into my hand and shouted: 'Krawiec, hitch up the horse, we're going to Rozwadów!'"

So, he quickly hitched up the horse, jumped on the cart and drove up to the barrack, where Mrs. Kosiński with Henio and Jurek where already waiting on the

---

* German lands east of the Oder-Neisse line ceded to Poland under the Potsdam Treaty of 1945.

doorstep along with apparently hastily packed bundles, valises. They threw everything onto the cart, seated the children, climbed in themselves, and off they went!

Krawiec drove as fast as he could, but they kept telling him to go faster, so he cracked the whip, urged on the horse!

They didn't tell him what had happened, of course, and Krawiec, who was hardly more than a boy, didn't dare to ask. But he sensed that something was wrong, that they were running away!

He drove them to where they wanted to go, to Rozwadów, to Kania, whom they had met at Warchoł's. Kania often used to come to Dąbrowa, where he sold pork. They didn't stay long, however. Kania later said that it was only overnight. They took the morning train for Łódź -- they were in a big hurry.

Franciszek Żiarno of Dąbrowa, who lived not far from the Kosińskis, saw that after their departure some types from the forest once again paid a visit to the barrack, but no one knows who they were. In those days it was better not to know.

* * *

Edward Warchoł only remembers that the "old man" suddenly rushed into the kitchen, threw the keys down on the table, and ran out. Mrs. Kosiński didn't even come in but remained sitting on Krawiec's cart. Though they had spent nearly two and a half years here, from September 1942 to April 1945, they didn't even say "good-bye" to Mrs. Warchoł, for Warchoł then was already behind bars.

They didn't say good-bye to anyone, for with whom could they take leave?

All of those with whom they had had close contacts, who had helped them the most, were now keeping company with the polar bears! There was village administrator Stępak, who had hidden the professor in the bean field, had shielded him with his office. And Adam Szkutnik of Wola, from whom Kosiński used to buy meat. Józef Gugataof Dąbrowa, probably his most intimate neighbor, with whom he had often talked. Władystaw Pamuła of Wola, who -- at the request of Father Okoń -- had drawn up identity papers for all the Kosiriskis.

* * *

To this day no one knows who "visited" them then. Was it the Home Army? The People's Guard? Be that as it may, literally on the day after the Kosińskis had "high tailed it" out of there, on 30 April, the People's Guard boys held a "dressing-down" for the officials of the new government, in particular for the organizers of the upcoming first of May celebrations.

Though they had weapons, they only ridiculed and humiliated the *apparatchiks.* They burst into houses, dragged out the quaking "commies," pulled down their pants and gave them a good caning on their bare fannies. Among the recipients of this dubious distinction were Jan P., the "red" village·administrator, and nearly all of his fellow "red" village administrators. The village administrator of Rzeczyca Okrągła managed to escape, hide out, so they seized his wife, tore off her dress, pulled down herpanties.

Kosiński was lucky, he had "taken it on the lam" in the nick of time, he didn't even get his "lumps" like most of the active "Pinkos" did.

And he surely would have taken a "licking," if only for the Red Army uniform in which he had dressed and constantly flaunted Henio, rubbing people the wrong way and tempting the furies!

* * *

After the war Rysiek Bogucki of Rzeczyca Okrągła with his parents moved to Puławy, and even before this to Łódź, where he just happened to bump into the professor at the train station. And as befits a former pupil, he greeted his mentor, walked up to him, and asked him how things were going. The professor clearly wasn't overjoyed to see him, but only wanted to know if this really was a chance encounter or whether the village had sent him. Then he muttered "good-bye" and scurried off.

It was very probably from Tracz people teamed that the professor and his famiJy had moved to Jelenia Góra. Tracz had enlisted in the army there and ran into the Kosińskis on the street. He told people about this after he came home on leave.

Rudolf Magryś, a blacksmith from Dąbrowa, who had lived beside Warchoł's barracks, made a trip to Jelenia Góra at that time. According to his wife -- to check out the job possibilities and opportunities opening in the Regained Territories. Dąbrowa, however, believes that he went there to find out what Kosiński was up to; he "had it in for" Kosiński, because he was sure that the professor had helped the Soviets arrange "long vacations" for his friends and neighbors.

And he later told people that he went up to the "old man" on the street, greeted him politely, reminded him who he was, but the professor pretended not to know him and "hot footed it" out of there like greased lightning!

Magryś came home; he somehow hadn't been able to find work, even though there was a big labor shortage there at the time -- in the socialist labor brigade, in the young men's Service to Poland laborbrigade.

It was from Magryś that Antoni Madurski of Dąbrowa, who also had thoughts of moving to the Regained Territories, obtained Kosiński's address. So he went to Jelenia Góra and phoned the professor. Madurski wasn't sure if the professor would want to talk with him, but the professor immediately invited him over; he had always been on good terms with Madurski -- he had talked old man Madurski out of joining the PWP, and young Madurski had driven the professor to Tarnobrzeg.

The professor received him warmly, asked him about news from the village. Mrs. Kosiński even served up some hors d'oeuvres, while Henio and Jurek popped up from time to time in the background. Kosiński was a director of one of the Jelenia Góra plants; he and his family lived in a well-appointed villa with a garden, and apparently were pretty well off.

Kosiński, of course, knew the director of *Celviscose,* and wrote a letter to him that was very helpful to Madurski -- he was hired on the spot. After that, he called Kosiński on the phone to thank him, and they never saw each other again.

Madurski is really the only person from the professor's old haunts whom the professor deigned to see, for whom he made an exception -- and it would be interesting to know why.

He may have been interested to know what was going on *there,* but he didn't ask.

* * *

There, in the meantime, in the spring of 1946, Warchoł was released from prison, and in 1947-1949 some *gulag* "guests" returned -- Pamuła and Szkutnik of Wola, Surma of Rzeczyca Okrągła. They were glad to be alive, to be able to live out their days with their families, under their own roofs. They were afraid to talk about what had happened to them, let alone think about revenge.

The more so as those who had "ratted" on them were no longer mere "commies"; they were now communists, the people's government, they occupied all of the posts -- government offices, the police, the security force; they had become district chairmen, village administrators, police superintendents -- who would dare let out apeep?

And who wanted to? It cannot be denied that the children of the former *gulag* inmates, not all of them, of course, also slowly began to join the "new order" -- they became members of the communist party, they wanted to come to terms with the authorities, on whom, especially in the countryside, everything depended permission to buy building materials, to build a house, to buy a tractor.

And it was probably only Szkutnik who still had a lot of vim and vigor left in him -- he got married again, was active in the peasants' movement, told everyone the truth straight to their faces. As a result, he served a few more jail sentences -- allegedly for concealing weapons in his barn, for contempt of the people's government.

* * *

Maybe that's why the new authorities wanted to "cleanse themselves" before him? On the occasion of St. John's Day several of those who had "denounced," who had "signed" (the names don't matter -- their children and grandchildren are living) suddenly dropped in on the father of Władysław Pamuła, also a former *gulag* inmate-- recalls Jan Szkutnik.

"Dear neighbors!" -- they said. – "What Judases or shades of Judases we are! We signed, but the Soviets 'ordered us to,' so what could we do? Would they listen

94

to us, boys with two years of formal schooling? But they listened to 'Kusiński' and asked his advice! For he was the brains of the party, a professor, the wisest man in the village! He wrote the 'accusations,' 'denounced,' 'fingered' people."

And they acted proud as peacocks, as though they hadn't done anything, for *he* had done it, not they!

Jan Szkutnik and his sister Bronisława Markut, also of Wola, recall how Jan Pamuła used to come to their father and often talk about this with him.

"Look here, pal," -- said Pamuła, for they were friends – "the communists are excusing themselves by blaming everything on 'Kusiński'! And yet their signatures were on the accusations that were read to us! So how can he be the one? We concealed him, and he betrayed us? For what? We lived in harmony together. No one did any harm to him."

And they even stopped talking about this, for it is unbelievable, absolutely preposterous!

Their own people had "turned them in," now their consciences were bothering them and they were blaming a completely innocent person?

✳ ✳ ✳

Though to tell the truth, people had reasons to suspect Kosiński.

For did he not at that time "cozy up" to those who took? Didn't he lose his head over them? Didn't he greet them with flowers? Didn't he dress Henio in a Red Army uniform? Perhaps -- like many people even wiser than he -- he believed in the "new order," in which there was no place for "enemies of the people" and "kulaks"? Maybe he didn't think that he was "stooling" but only helping?

Didn't he go around -- they added -- with the "Soviet top brass," who really set great store by his opinion, as the release of Temporale showed? And it would have been odd if in this matter of life or death Temporale hadn't asked the "brains of the party" for help. Sometimes even the biggest "numskulls" signed orders and not the most important or the smartest people.

Wasn't he also with the "commies," members of the PWP, which officially and openly collaborated with the Russians, and not only here? Its role has been judged indisputably.

And Warchoł, not a stupid man, who always maintained that he had seen Kosiński's handwriting on his accusation? And what about the "scholarly" style of the other accusations?

And the "Whites" came for him in April 1945, but he managed to escape. And after that he also ran away from the villagers -- from Rysiek Bogucki in Łódź, in Jelenia Góra from Magryś. And then after this neither he nor "junior" ever sent any news.

∗ ∗ ∗

Even though -- in Dąbrowa's opinion -- he consorted with the Soviet "brass," this does not necessarily mean that he "turned in" people. He may have joined the "commies" just to survive. To protect himself against those who wanted to strip him of his last gold, but it's strange that he did this so late, when everyone knew that he had no more money.

But even if this was so, why did he later remain silent? -- people wondered.

The more so as those to whom he owed the most were sent to Siberia - village administrator Stępak, Pamuła, Szkutnik. And Warchoł, who "only" went to jail.

However, he never sent word, never wrote, never visited them. He did not talk about this like a person. He didn't try to explain, to justify himself, and they would have believed everything, for they really wanted to.

The Soviets might have been blackmailing him, threatening him! They were the masters of life and death, the new occupiers. "You will go to Siberia and no one will find your grave" they often said. Or – *"Zhyt' budyesh, no... nye zakhochesh!"**

These were not idle threats, for they deported people, and in the Rzeszów prison there were more people than under the Germans.

The war had hardly ended, especially for the Jews. Maybe this was the price of their survival? The secret of the "old man" and then of the "young man," who carried it with him for his entire life?

---

* You will stay alive, but wish you weren't!

Or maybe the "old man" hated them? -- people also asked themselves. Maybe he wanted to get even, like many others did? Though he not been mistreated, he none the less had lived with "cap in hand," had lived at their pleasure, dependent on one word from them, on one Judas!

So he could finally lift up his head, get even, take his revenge. Make up for those unquestionably terrible years!

This doesn't surprise them at all. That's how things are in life. People feel resentment toward their benefactors, and often repay good with bad. Every time you lend someone money -- you have an enemy instead of a friend! You raise children -- then they become your worst enemies!

Dionizy Garbacz, co-author (with Andrzej Zagórski) of the book *In the Red Pincers* (Brzozów-Rzeszów, 1991) on the fate of the Home Army of the Rzeszów sub-district after the entry of the Red Army, is the most knowledgeable expert in the vicinity on this problem.

"These were the first deportations" -- he says – "and there were no documents, no records, no files. After this it was 'better,' more traces, but in those first ones -- they just loaded people in Black Marias and took them away, that's all."

The book contains a fist of persons taken to *gulags* from August 1944 to January 1945; and on this list are the names Stępak, Pamuła, Szkutnik, Surma -- "soldiers of the Home Army of the Tarnobrzeg district."

The authors compiled this list for many years on the basis of eye-witness accounts, Home Army reports, parish records, in which the names of the deported were sometimes recorded. The list is incomplete and is being constantly supplemented.

The list doesn't contain the names of all the victims, let alone the informers.

" ... *In most cases Poles themselves, as a rule those associated with the PWP, police, Security Force, were of great assistance to the NKVD.*"

How will we ever be able to learn today how things really were? -- they ask.

Is this at all possible?

The "young" generation is starting to die out, to say nothing of the "old" one.

So the only thing that is certain is that he left a bad memory of himself behind.

Be that as it may, he was with those who "took." And with those who "turned in," who assisted in this. With the Soviets and with the Polish Workers' Party members, and that's enough.

"He stayed alive and then ran away," though he "thought of himself as a professor" -- they all emphasize.

Even after many years, when emotions had died down, he never sent word in any way -- which pains them the most. He wasn't even interested in whether they were alive, in whether they had returned from Siberia, if Warchoł had been released from prison. Meanwhile, they knew that he hadn't left the country, that he was living in Poland.

All of this increased their suspicions that "there had been something," that he "had been involved," "was ashamed to face them."

* * *

So they tried to forget about him.

Not immediately, of course. In the first postwar years, when the *gulag* inmates started to return home and Warchoł was released from jail, they still mentioned him, talked about him.

But what could they do? These were only conjectures, suspicions. They were not thirsting for revenge or retaliation. At most they uttered:

"May God repay him in his children!"

"May He plague him in his children!"

And they surely uttered this in an evil hour.

* * *

Jan P., who in those times not only "snitched" on his neighbors but even led them personally to the Black Marias, was punished in his children. Though he is now old, decrepit, after his wife's death he lives alone, which in these parts is regarded as a misfortune, a scourge -- in old age one should be among one's children, grandchildren.

Though he has several children, none of them wants to take him in or come to visit him. They know what he was like, what people say about him. He sits there alone like an eagle owl. "He's atoning for his sins" -- people say.

God sometimes waits a long time but punishes severely.

* * *

Father Jan Butrym, the local parish-priest, who is about to leave, does not deny that he didn't have things easy here. Not only because since a long time this has been "red" territory, with many unbelievers, secular funerals, etc.

The tragedy which the local people experienced still makes itself felt today. Not every day, of course, but sometimes echoes of it are heard in the most unexpected situations. For instance, someone says that he's not going to remodel the church with this one or that one, for he is the son of a traitor! And that one in tum accuses others! and they -- point the finger at "old man" Kosiński!

So he must have heard about the suspicions people voiced about him. It's surprising, though, that they expressed these suspicions to a woman reporter. For to this day they bear the mark of "that person." They are mistrustful, are afraid of being betrayed again, of revenge and Siberia. "Solidarity" arose here very late, after all of Poland already belonged to it.

The cup of gall was probably overfilled by the "young one," who never mentioned them, never admitted publicly that he had known them. He did not come to see them. What is more, he turned them away when they came to see him. This pained them very much, touched them to the quick.

Perhaps it was he who reopened the old wound?

CHAPTER 10

Young Kusiński

Years passed, it seemed that the chapter called "Kosiński" had been closed a long time ago. But when, sometime in 1968, when bad things were being written about Jews, someone read, someone heard on the radio, that Jurek "Kusiński", the little black bird that used to hang on the fence all the time, had written a book! Seems it was called *Blue Bird*, with calumnies about those who hid Jews during the war.

But they did not take much notice of it at the time, did not get upset. After all, it could not have had a connection to them. After all, he survived the occupation sitting pretty and had no complaints to make. Perhaps he wrote about the time he spent outside of Dąbrowa? He arrived in 1942, but as far as they knew, things had not gone badly for him before that. He arrived tidy, well cared for, so it could not have been otherwise.

Perhaps they had heard more about his *Blue Bird*, but in sum not much at all. Moreover, no one had read his book, no one saw it, and more importantly – who then believed in what the papers wrote?

Therefore, they were happy that he became a writer, that is *a somebody*! Their effort and the risk they took were not wasted. They preserved an exceptional person! And this was probably proof that they took good care of him – he did not go bad but weaned to adulthood on the milk they provided.

"Dąbrowa saved him, Kępa fed him, even fattened him!" they said with pride.

Then for a few years it was quiet, and only during *Solidarity* times did they read and hear more about him again. But this time all good! He was known in the world, but not here, where the *Blue Bird* and his other books were not printed.

Then in April of 1988 he suddenly came to Poland for a short stay and they saw him on television!

The first impression – a spitting image of his mother. Over the years he grew to resemble her even more. As for his *old man*, not a visible smidgen! The *old man*, before he went to seed and became a *Bolshie*, was a serious man, stately. He spoke little, but wisely with dignity, weighing every word.

The young one talked like a machine gun, jumped from subject to subject, side stepped questions, but said what he wanted. He would not look his interlocutors in the eye, but with a glassy gaze, looked ahead or over people's heads, thus not making a good impression on the viewers.

What was most important was how he spoke about Poles and Jews, the need for Polish-Jewish understanding, but he never mentioned the villagers. He did not acknowledge them or give them a "leg-up" – not even with a single word. He never sent them greetings, like saying "Dąbrowa Rzyczyska, my thanks to you!"

That would have been enough, he did not have to mention names, perhaps Warchoł, because he deserved it.

They did not know *The Painted Bird* and assumed that it was something written by the *old man*.

And who could have blamed the young snot nosed kid for anything? Who would drag anything out if he came there like royalty? He had lived through the same bad times as they, and it would have been enough to forget about anything bad in the past, and just hug one another after all those years!

But he slipped by like a shooting star and disappeared, left the country and that was it.

The second visit was announced well ahead of time. Edward Warchol and his brother-in-law, Bronisław Wołoszyn, read about it in the afternoon paper. The article said that on April 21, 1989, the Warsaw *Czytelnik* bookstore on Wiejska Street would host a book signing for his *Painted Bird*. They decided to go there themselves, for from his actions during the first visit they had no faith that he would remember them at all.

Of course, they thought about it, if they should? After all that had happened? But he was an innocent, a child, perhaps he didn't even know anything? Did the parents tell him? Perhaps he forgot the name of the village? And if he did, how would he behave toward them? Would he show gratitude? Would he invite them to come to America? Or even buy them a vodka at the Marriott Hotel? In any case, they wanted to see him, to talk, buy *The Painted Bird*, about which they heard such worrisome things.

The story of their meeting with Young Kusiński is now known by the entire vicinity. Everyone was curious, and they repeated it many times, and they told it to me again.

They dressed elegantly, that is in suit and tie, taking the night train, kidding each other along the way that now they have one foot in America already, because Jurek will surely invite them for a visit! In the morning they arrived in Warsaw and bought flowers, took a cab to Wiejska Street, else they might not have found the place. They were there before eight in the morning, thinking that they would be first. But there already was a long queue before the book shop, which apparently had been growing since four in the morning.

As time went by the queue grew and grew, numbering eventually several thousand persons, stretching out into the nearby streets as far as Three Crosses Square. Immediately an organizing committee went into action, which handed out numbers. Edward got 305 and his brother-in-law 306.

They had never seen anything like this before. There were TV crews from around the globe, press, radio, an elegant crowd, and cops to keep order! And all of this, because of them! Old Warchoł, Dąbrowa, the entire village! One word during the occupation would have crashed the whole thing and there would have been no Kosiński or this crowd. But despite this they stood in line with the others, hanging on to their numbers, without which they would not get admittance.

Just before eleven there were shouts that he was coming, and many ran toward the curb. Bronisław Wolłszyn kept his place in line, fearing that they may not be allowed to come back in. But Edward Warchoł ran with the crowd and stood by a *Ruch* newsstand. He was in luck! A long black limousine with an American flag on it pulled up and Jurek Kosiński jumped out. He was just as he was in Dąbrowa, only older. The lucky ones near him, greeted him, shook his hand. They yelled something. Edward Warchoł, found himself among these people, shouted as well.

"I'm Warhoł from Dąbrowa, do you recognize me?"

Jurek only nodded his head and then moved on, or rather was swept along by his retinue into the interior of the *Czytelnik* book store.

They saw that conditions for a conversation were not good. He was signing his book and exchanging but a few words with each person. The line pushed along, governed by the organizing committee, which would not allow anyone to get extra time with the author. So they wrote on a card, introducing themselves, and asked for a conversation. They handed it to him after their numbers were called out and were allowed to approach the table.

Meanwhile, he was receiving dozens of business cards, invitations, letters and the like. He did not even look at the card, but passed it on along with the others to his handlers. There might have been two ladies and two men there. One of the women, it was said in the line, was his wife. Edward Warchoł introduced himself again.

"Good day, Mr. Jurek!" he said, though in the past they addressed each other informally. "I am Edward Warchoł from Dąbrowa Rzeczycka, son of Andrzej, in whose house you and your parents sheltered during the occupation!" And he extended his hand.

Kosiński shook it, but coldly and officiously, without a hint of a smile. He did not get up, to greet them in a more heartfelt manner. Instead he gazed at them with an ice-cold stare and in a similar tone said, "My parents are deceased!" (This sounded as if he had wanted nothing to do with them.)

"But our mother, thank God, is still alive though she is over eighty years-old," continued Warchoł unfazed. Kosiński passed over this with silence, did not give any regards to be conveyed, though the woman was old and ill, and would die a month later.

"Only my brother is still alive," he said finally, breaking the silence.

"Your brother?" said Warchoł unnecessarily, losing valuable time, but he remembered that little Henio was not the Kosiński's natural child, something they did not hide.

"Yes, my brother, I will go to see him in Łódź,"* he said. Then he signed a copy of *The Painted Bird* that they had bought. They had hoped he would give them a copy but somehow, he had not arrived at that idea. For a moment, that seemed like an eternity, they stood without saying a word. They were unnerved and tired,

---

* Mr. Henry Kosinski lives in Łódź and has no desire to have any conversations about Jerzy, or the Kosinski family. No, simply not. I must understand this. (Author's Note)

while he – always so eloquent – apparently had no desire to carry on a conversation.

Yet, luck smiled upon them. The lady sitting nearby had read their card, and asked something of him, with great interest.

"Jurek, these people sheltered you during the war?"

"Yes!" he retorted. She said something in English to the other persons in the retinue, who then peppered him with questions, but in English. The Poles understood only the name "*Jerry, Jerry.*"

Then the only nice moment of the visit occured. Kosiński's wife rose and smiling motioned them over with her hand to come to the table, where places were found for them. Then she asked him something in English, but he was angry and displeased. He answered her sharply and made a gesture that communicated rejection.

"Write down your addresses!" he said quickly. "I will write to you soon! I will make a visit!"

Of course, they wrote it on a card that he put in his pocket. Then he extended his hand, still unsmiling.

"Good bye!" he said, and they replied, "Good bye, Mr. Jurek!"

They wanted to say something more, but what? And how to say it? The organizing committee was making noise that they were taking up too much time, scandalous behavior! Everyone had their rights!

They returned sad and depressed. They had wrongly thought that he would greet them in a heartfelt way or that he would not forget to send greetings to their mother or the entire village. He didn't even bother to inquire how they were and what they were doing, or how their lives were going? Perhaps they were in need of something? But no warm words were spoken. He made no friendly gesture. Instead, it seemed that he wanted to be quickly rid of them! And in *The Painted Bird*, he only signed his name, nothing more.

It's a miracle that he even admitted knowing them, for he could have said as bold as brass -- what Warchoł? What Dąbrowa? I don't know you! But how could he be sure that the entire village wasn't waiting in front of the *Czytelnik* bookstore with pitchforks? He was probably afraid that they would make a commotion -- start shouting, telling, substantiating, and reporters, radio, television were all around! He preferred to get rid of them politely and quietly, promising that he would write and come!

They, of course, were angry at themselves for not acting differently, for not saying at least -- How is this, Mr. Jurek? Aren't you even going to offer us a cup of tea? But they were tired, nervous -- they had traveled all night and then had stood in line for so many hours. It's fortunate that they said anything at all, and they were banking mainly on him, everything depended on how he would behave. And since he didn't want to know them -- it couldn't be helped, they had their pride. They had their homes, farms, children and grandchildren, and didn't have to ask him for anything.

They still hoped that he would write, come, but nothing of the kind! Following this, he never mentioned them in any of the interviews which he gave everywhere, not even on Television News!

What is more, many of their neighbors laughed at them that "Kusiński," this time the young one, had duped them again. As usual, he had weaseled out again! Most of the villagers, however, commiserated with them, thought that he shouldn't have sent them "packing" like that!

That smart, educated man on television? A writer, how could that be?

Antoni Madurski of Dąbrowa Rzeczyca, a retired colonel of the Polish Army who since a long time has resided in Warsaw, also wanted to see him. Mainly to talk about *The Painted Bird,* because, as a neighbor from Dąbrowa, he had felt humiliated and offended by the book. So he came to Wiejska Street, but rather late -- he hadn't expected such crowds -- and took a place almost at the end of the line.

After a few hours he was fed up with waiting, really with inching forward step by step. Even more so -- with the crowd, which he soon concluded had come just out of curiosity. The people who made up the crowd knew nothing about Kosiński except that he had made a career in the West. They hadn't read any of his books, for how could they have? And they wanted to buy *The Painted Bird* only because "everyone else was buying it." So he had enough of this, he couldn't wait any longer.

However, before he left, he wrote a letter to Kosiński. He introduced himself -- said he was a former neighbor from Dąbrowa Rzeczyca and hoped that Kosiński remembered this name. He expressed the wish to meet with him, to talk about the *Bird*. He was interested to know why there were only bad things in it, since as a child Kosiński had experienced mostly good things. Why had he never mentioned Dąbrowa publicly? Hadn't it occurred to him that the village was waiting for this?

He signed the letter, gave his address and telephone number. He *gave* the letter to someone standing in front of him, who promised to deliver it, saying that he was determined to wait his tum. No one knows, of course, whether this person kept his word; in any case, Kosiński didn't call or write.

Madurski really wasn't expecting that he would -- in front of the *Czytelnik* bookstore he ran into Edward Warchoł and his brother-in-law, who had just come out of the bookstore and made no secret of how they had been received. And since Kosiński had treated the son of the man who had hid him in such a way, would he treat only a neighbor any better?

Henryk Kosiński, Jerzy Kosiński's step-brother, lives in Łódź; he is a doctor.

Despite many requests, he has refused to be interviewed.

"I don't want to talk about him" - he explained on the telephone. "I lost contact with him a long time ago, we went our separate ways. He went to America and completely forgot about me; he never wrote a word, never invited me."

They did see each other in Łódź, during Jerzy Kosiński's second visit to Poland in 1989, but this was in a crowd and in passing, during an official meeting at city hall, where, in addition to local VIPs, there many other acquaintances of Jerzy, all of whom tried to get to see him and exchange a few words with him. As a result, Jerzy and his step-brother only had a brief conversation, after which -- attended by journalists and photographers - they went to the communal cemetery to the graves of Mr. and Mrs. Kosiński. From there the famous author hurried off to his next meeting.

Why does Henryk speak of the "Kosińskis"? After all, they were his parents or step-parents. That's unfortunately how things turned out; these are very difficult and complicated matters. To be sure, Henryk was fed, clothed, went to college, but ... is that enough? On the surface, all of this looked perfectly in order, but there had never been any warm feelings or kindliness. It was always Jurek and Jurek. Henio had always been in the shade, had always been someone worse.

After the death of Mr. Kosiński in 1962, Mrs. Kosiński moved to Warsaw, where Henryk used to see her once a year. He was left alone in Łódź, even though at that time he was still only a college student and needed a home and care.

Henryk remembers nothing from his wartime experiences; he was only 3-4-years-old then. He only knows that he spent the war years with the Kosińskis in some Polish village, but he doesn't know the name, for they never mentioned it. No, he was never there, he doesn't know where that is -- and why these questions?

He knows very little about the Kosinskis, at most a few facts. She, from the house of Weinreich, an only child, her parents died before the war, she graduated from music school and played the piano, but never in public, only at home. She was intelligent, she knew languages, after the war she worked in various offices, but exactly where, he does not remember. Kosiński, however, before the war I think was a businessman, he also lectured - that's why he was called a professor - in a business college . After the war he worked in unions and in general in high positions - he was educated, knew languages, traveled and he could have his pick. He had a brother who had emigrated to America before the war, he was a naval officer, he sailed on ships, he got married late and he did not have children, he died quite a long time ago.

Mrs. Kosiński visited her son in America; she also met with him in Amsterdam and gave him all of the family photos and mementos. And that's enough. He doesn't want to say anything more about this, I should understand that.

Mrs. Kosiński visited her son in America; she also met with him in Amsterdam and gave him all of the family photos and mementos. Maybe there is something also with Hania? For many years she had been the Kosińskis' maid, almost a member of the family, and in Mrs. Kosiński's last years her nurse, to whom Mrs. Kosiński bequeathed her apartment.

And that's enough. He doesn't want to say anything more about this, I should understand that.

* * *

Mrs. Hanna G. still lives in the Warsaw apartment of Elżbieta Kosiński at Belwederska Street. She absolutely refuses to speak about the Kosińskis. "Oh, it's you again?" -- she says and immediately slams down the receiver.

* * *

After they returned from Warsaw, Edward Warchoł and his brother-in-law tried to read *The Painted Bird.* Several neighbors from Dąbrowa, who worked in Stalowa Wola, also bought or borrowed the book, leafed through it. So most of the villagers know the book, but almost no one has read it from cover to cover -- they couldn't. The rest of the people only "heard" aboutit.

And then they raised the roof!

Let the wolf in, and he'll eat you! - they said.

He never even mentioned them, he sent the Warchołs packing not only on account of the "old man" but on account of his book! After this book could he look them in the face? It's odd that he came at all, that he wasn't afraid.

To be sure, in a "scholarly," difficult to fathom introduction he supposedly explained that the action takes place in a "mythical land," "existing nowhere." That the action has no place -- no name of the country, even less so of the village, no last names, no concrete facts! This is an explanation good for everybody else, but not for them! How can this be a mythical land when it is exactly the same as Dąbrowa and the vicinity? Hardly changed in the slightest?

The action of the *Bird* takes place in several adjacent villages, just as the story of the Kosińskis. They lived in Dąbrowa, but went to church in Wola. Kępa fed them, Rzeczyca Okrągła concealed them during operations and man-hunts, Rzeczyca, like everyone else, was silent for a long time.

The landscape of the book is mainly Dąbrowa -- like the villages in the *Bird* it is situated next to extensive forests, in which -- as in the book – "a local Jew was hiding," who in reality was Karol Liebeskind. There were "deserted military bunkers with thick walls of reinforced concrete," not so much full of rats as of ordinary moles. The "white" and "red" partisans were fighting, and the "Whites" took revenge on all people suspected of helping the "Reds," who in tum punished villages that helped the "Whites"; and sometimes "both groups attacked and murdered each other."[*]

And -- as in Dąbrowa – "railroad tracks ran along the edge of the forest" and -- as in the *Bird* -- along these tracks traveled military transports and cattle-cars bearing Jews to Majdanek. Dąbrowa, like the peasants in the *Bird,* ran out to watch them. But not out of curiosity or to "wave cheerfully to the engineer," but to find out what was going on -- whom they were transporting this time and to where. There were no newspapers, radio, or television, and the tracks served as a source of information. So the villagers ran to watch, but in horror, with a heavy heart, for they knew that after the Jews it would be their tum! Little "Kusiński" also ran to watch -- Warchoł's barracks were not far from the tracks.

In neighboring Kępa there was also a railroad bridge over the river San that was guarded day and night by the Germans, just as in the *Bird,* where: "Near the village a railroad bridge spanned steep rocky slopes, between them a river flowed through a wide river-bed.... Soldiers in helmets kept guard next to cannons, and the angular sign of the swastika, sewn on a flag hanging down from the top of the steel structure, twisted in the wind."

In Dąbrowa there were and still are "bogs and quagmires," though hardly as "vast" and "menacing" as the author exaggerated in the *Bird.* The locals who are familiar with them cross, or rather jump over, them without problems.

Dąbrowa also had and has "poor soil"; before the war it was "poor and squalid" -- a *morga*[*] of sand was really something -- and that's why people didn't raise cows but -- like the villagers in the *Bird* -- goats and rabbits, which would eat anything. "Underfed," like them, Dąbrowa also "greeted with joy the time of mushroom-picking" -- for the village lived not only off the sandy soil but off the forest

-- mushrooms, raspberries, blueberries.

It is also hard to deny that the village was "backward," even though it had a four-grade schoolhouse, the upper grades and the grammar-school, which were

---

[*] All quotations from *Malowany Ptak,* "Czytelnik," Warsaw 1992

[*] A unit of land measure ($= 5,600\,m^2$).

attended by children of the more affluent peasants, were in nearby Radomyśl and Rozwadów. In fact, however, most of the adults couldn't read or write, treated illnesses with herbs, leeches, "charms" -- not out of ignorance but because they couldn't afford a doctor.

And, as in the *Bird,* "they didn't know electricity" and "beaten tracks were rare." "The cottages were built from logs, covered on both sides by mud mixed with straw. The walls sunken deep into the ground held up thatched roofs crowned with chimneys made of clay and willow withes."

Moreover, as in the *Bird,* the village was "remote," "isolated from the world," though this is somewhat of an exaggeration -- not far away were Radomyśl, Rozwadów, Stalowa Wola. Until the times of the partisan operations, it really was a small, quiet haven; before the war there were only thirty some odd numbers, "homesteads" as people say here.

The people also may very well have been "dark," "extremely superstitious," "speaking a strange dialect," "not understanding the language of the educated class which the Boy spoke" -- dark-haired, dark-eyed, swarthy -- like "little Kusiński."

But what is probably most important -- they were decent, god-fearing, honest. Why otherwise would they have taken such a risk for a Jewish family that they didn't know and wasn't from here? Why would they have kept this family -- unselfishly -- for two and a halfyears?

✳ ✳ ✳

In the *Bird* there is an almost identical character from Dąbrowa -- the bird fancier Lech, whose archetype was unquestionably Kosińskis' neighbor -- Lech Tracz. He still lives in a cottage covered with cages full of birds. He, too, like the character in the book, "was drawn to the woods." He, too, "spent his youth in forests among birds," which he has loved since he was a child. He set snares for them, caught them, and then let them go; sometimes he painted them with lime, for where could one get paint during the occupation?

He mostly painted crows, which were the most numerous. Especially for the local children, who didn't have toys or any special entertainments, but also for himself. He is crazy, but not dangerous -- everyone likes him and feels sorry for him that "little Kusiński" didn't even bother to change his name, for now someone is always asking him: where is stupid Ludmiła?

Kosiński also apparently remembered Labina, who did housework for his family. One of the female characters of the *Bird* has almost the same name, that is, Łabina, who also "went to the richer farmers to work as a maid." Labina was also often called tabina, her son -- Łaba, which is one of the more common surnames here; the maiden name of the wife of Józef Stępak from Dąbrowa and Kępa under the Germans -- was also Laba.

Sefania Labina (1910) was Kosińskis' maid; she still lives in Dąbrowa, but she is old and sick. Laba, her husband, who was by no means handsome, was killed on the railroad tracks about twenty years ago, and spiteful people now badger her by asking whether he really was "red" like the one in the book.

In the *Bird* there are a lot of local names, maybe not so many from Dąbrowa as from the vicinity. Tęcza, for instance, or Makar, whose name was well-known here at once time. Makar of nearby Kuryłówka suffocated in a house burned down by the Soviets during an operation against the "white" partisans.

The *Bird* also speaks of "Lilka, a Jewish girl" put in the care of one of the peasants, who "beat her and raped her, forced her to engage in various shameful acts, and in the end she disappeared." Yet, Lilka was the first name of a Jewish girl taken in for a few months by the Migdałeks -- the Kosińskis' neighbors in the barrack. "Little Kusiński" sometimes played with her, but no one beat her or raped her. On the contrary, she was sent from one family to another and survived the war. People say that she lives in Israel. Dąbrowa was one of the stages of her wartime wandering.

There is also a priest in the story -- a carbon copy of Father "Okuń, "who brought the Kosińskis to Dąbrowa. Like the real priest, he was "small, plump, dressed in a frayed, faded cassock." Kindly and good, always coming to the Boy's aid, he places him under the care of one of the peasants, then visits and watches over him, as Father "Okuń" watched over his charges.

There is also a "local Jew hiding in the vicinity," in fact Karol Liebeskind, whom also "the entire village knew, since his grandfather had been the owner of a large landed estate"; in reality, a saw-mill. And in fact, "everyone liked him; people said: a Jew, but a decent person."

Also, as in reality -- there was an adopted brother. Except that in the *Bird* the Boy meets him only after he is reunited with his parents. Meanwhile, little Henio had already come with them to Dąbrowa with his nanny. And, like the little brother in the *Bird,* he was "a four-year-old boy, an orphan, saved by his aged nanny in the third year of the war."

There are good Germans, who save the Boy's life twice -- an elegant, "superhuman" officer and a soldier, who didn't shoot the Boy in the forest, but told him to run away. And in fact, "Kusiński" always encountered such Germans -- the "old man" in the state purchasing center, in Kępa, where he ran into the chief of the Gestapo himself, and "old lady Kusiński" and "little Kusiński" at the house of village administrator Stępak. And on every Sunday, during Holy Mass in the church in Wola, which the Germans also attended and took communion. They stood by the altar, the "Kusińskis" by the entrance, but -- no matter -- it was under the same roof!

There is an entire mass of Dąbrowa details, facts that could be multiplied.

If only his own fire, or the smoke-bombs, which in the *Bird* -- for some unknown reason -- he called comets. These were empty tin cans, punctured on the sides, filled with sawdust and attached to a wire, which made it possible to swing them like a lasso. They didn't serve at all, as he exaggerated, "for survival" but for fun. The boys grazing cows used them to light fires, bake potatoes.

As in the book, they also played with "dangerous soap," that is, with military hardware found in the forest -- with rifle cartridges or land mines." Both the real boys and the boys in the book skated on "sickle-shaped" skates -- hand-made skates fashioned from reaping hooks and wood and fastened to their shoes; they also tied "sails" to their backs -- a piece of canvas, thanks to which they could race with the wind.

* * *

There are scenes which really did take place, but the author painted them in black colors, "spiced" themwith atrocities, which did not happen.

Young Kosiński did indeed serve for a time as an altar boy and during one mass did drop the missal, but for this no one threw him into latrine, causing him to lose his speech.

It is true that the local boys, as boys will be, grabbed him a few times, tried to pull down his pants to see his "bird," but just out of curiosity. But this never happened. Somehow Jurek always managed to get away. And no one on such an occasion -- as happened to the Boy in the *Bird* -- tried to drown him in an air-hole, no one beat him.

In fact, "on one fine morning from the water they pulled out an enormous sheatfish with long, prominent whiskers. This was a powerful fish of enormous dimensions." To this day they remember it -- it was caught by old Tracz -- and, as in the *Bird,* the entire village ran down to see it, even "little Kusiński"!

But, like everyone else, he just stood there and watched. No one threw him into the water -- as happened to the Boy -- no one tried to drown him, throwing stones at him in the bargain!

* * *

There are entire chapters that are almost identical with everything that happened in Dąbrowa.

For instance, the onslaught on the Kalmucks, who -- as in the *Bird* -- arrived after the departure of the Germans and were "dressed in green, German uniforms with shiny buttons and field-caps pulled down to their eyes." They also "plundered and raped," though mostly in neighboring Rzeczyca Okrągła. Dąbrowa, including the Kosińskis, had run off to the forest, waited out the onslaught; just the windows in the barrack were smashed in.

And the chapters about the entry of the Red Army? It came, as in the *Bird,* when "summer was ending, sheaves of wheat were standing in rows in the fields." The Soviets were greeted by boys carrying red flags, on which "hammers and sickles" had been clumsily drawn. Among the welcomers was "old man" Kosiński, who was just as enthralled by the Red Army as the Boy in the *Bird,* who became -- like little Henio -- the son of the regiment in a Red Anny soldier's uniform. He made friends with the soldier Mitka, with the political officer Gavril, just as the "old man" had with the Soviet "top brass."

* * *

So -- for at least some of the local people -- how can this be a "mythical land" which "cannot be found on the map?"

This is Dąbrowa, but without the sadism, perversions, atrocities.

CHAPTER 11

The Ugly Black Bird

And into Dąbrowa -- railroad tracks, bunkers, smoke-bombs, the bird-fancier Lech, Labina -- he inserted wild beasts in human skin. Sadists who tried to drown a child in a latrine, set dogs on him, who hung people, gouged out their eyes with a spoon. Hyenas lying in wait for transports of Jews. Perverts copulating with goats, rabbits. Murderers of stupid Ludmita!

For everyone this is only a book, a story, a "fable," but not for them. They had a right to take it to heart, didn't they? To feel "described," "smeared"? For since all of the details are from Dąbrowa, then aren't the people from there also?

To tell the truth, since he had turned them into savages, they all should have grabbed their pitchforks, gotten into a motor-coach, and gone to confront him in Warsaw, asking him loudly:

"Hey, you snot-nose!" -- though he is no longer alive, for them he is still small or young. "What does this mean? You are a writer? Couldn't you put your butchers in some mountains? On the coast? Change their last names?"

And ask him, how could he do this? Repay them this like this?

After all, on television they see Jews who come to Poland, pay visits, lavish gifts on people -- renovate homes, report to newspapers, to Jerusalem, for a medal! They don't want anything from him, let him go with God, it's not for thankfulness that they concealed him! But let him at least not "blacken" them, not "describe" them!

The more so as no harm came to him, he was snug as a bug in a rug, as hardly any other Jewish child -- are they supposed to tell this once again?

Of course he was afraid, but only he? The entire village would have been burned to the ground -- they, their children, all their possessions.

There is no desire for revenge or retaliation in their hearts. He's lucky he came upon them, for the highlanders would never have let him get away with it; they would have even gotten him in America. While these people are no angels, they are quiet, god-fearing, decent, and that's why he took such liberties!

If they were like those persons described in the book, they would have refused Father Okoń -- why would they need such trouble? Or they would have taken Jurek in so they could "double-cross" him for a kilogram of sugar or a liter of grain alcohol, which was what the Germans paid for one Jew. There were rogues, but not among them; the best proof is that the Kosińskis survived here for two and a half years!

Moreover, the debaucheries with which everyone now reproaches them also never happened. Poverty yes, but not scenes like in the book! In a miserable, god-forsaken, prewar village?

Would a country woman who had to take care of the house, yard, and fields still have had the energy and time for that? And a peasant who every day had to walk fifteen kilometers one way to the mill and then after that work in the fields? At most, on Sunday he "possessed" his wife, performed his conjugal duty, that's all. And he never even saw her naked, for all of this took place in the dark, as God instructed.

＊＊＊

They sometimes wondered what had entered him. Was it some evil demon?

Maybe this was on account of the "old man"? For the sentence that had been passed on him? For their flight from Dąbrowa?

Maybe he also -- like the "old man" -- hated them? And he finally wanted to get even, to make up for those unquestionably terrible years, if only for the "bird" which they had tried to see and which must have been such a big shock for the young master?

Or maybe it was only "for America," which they also know, for they have worked there illegally. He wanted to rise in the world, to make a career, but

America is America, and a lot of strange things happen there! So he invented these "fables" and inserted them in Dąbrowa, for he remembered that place best. How could he imagine that communism would collapse? That his book would come out in Polish? That he would stand face toface with Edward Warchoł?

He floundered, got confused, and then the moment was lost -- he couldn't look them in the face.

Or maybe it was his sick imagination? An unbalanced mind? But that's not their fault, it's his parents'!

Perhaps they were wrong in just keeping him in the house or in the yard, not letting him play with the local boys. Of course, they were afraid for him, but they quickly came to realize that nothing threatened them from the village. And so from time to time he could have played with the local lads, have invited them to his house. He would have understood that they were not monsters, and they -- that he was just like any other boy. They might have even seen his "bird," and after that there wouldn't have been secrets, fights, scraps.

But he played at most with the children of Migdałek the teacher, never with the local boys. Most of the time, however, he just hung on the fence like an ugly black bird, watched over his "organ," and nothing good came out of this. "He got a screw loose," "he became abnormal," "his mind became twisted," and after this he probably never straightened out.

For how otherwise could he have "described" them like that? Have "smeared" them? Have made them objects ofridicule?

Mrs. Emila Stec of Rzeczyca Okrągła, Jan Pamuła's sister, was once talking with friends about Kosiński and, of course, bragged that she knew him -- she had spent the occupation in these parts, his father had taught her brother. But they absolutely refused to believe her; they looked at her suspiciously -- after all, he had wandered, they heard, through the Ukraine, had never mentioned any Rzeczyca or Dąbrowa -- was it there that he had lost his speech?

While waiting in front of the *Czytelnik* bookstore Warchoł and his brother-in-law also mentioned that they had sheltered the Kosińskis in Dąbrowa Rzeczycka, but they quickly held their tongue, for everyone started to laugh and poke fun at them. What Kosińskis, since he had wandered alone? And all around him inhuman, ignorant savages -- were they some of them?

Mr. Stefan Kochan, a native of Rzeczyca Okrągła, admits that he is hardly a local patriot. He doesn't like his native parts -- typical Galician poverty, with all its envy, cupidity, unfriendliness, communism, which had its supporters here and there. No comparison with the warm, kindly Polaks among whom he spent several years before the war.

To tell the truth, he always wondered why the locals had behaved this way during the occupation. With no thought of gain they had concealed not only the Kosińskis but also Karol Liebeskind. They also looked the other way when the teacher Migdałek kept two out-of-town Jewish children in his home.

Despite this, today they cannot even say that they knew the Kosińskis; proudly say, look here -- we harbored not just anybody!

People immediately quip -- this they have experienced this time and again -- that they are fibbing, pretending, making themselves out to be heroes. For why otherwise, did Kosiński never acknowledge them publicly? Maybe they have confused him with somebody else? Do they have any proof?

Yet, there is one indisputable piece of evidence -- a photo of the professor in front of the state purchasing center in Dąbrowa, a picture taken by Mr. Kochan, a clear and successful photo; sitting next to the professor is Adam Latawiec, who also worked there.

Apart from this, there are only the memories of old, prewar people. But the memories of many of them, for the Kosińskis never really hid; the "old man" was too active, so a lot of people remember him.

He is remembered not only by residents of Dąbrowa, Kępa, Wola Rzeczycka, Rzeczycka Długa but also by those who "made it" -- by those who became educated and left. Jan Pamuła of Stalowa Wola, Stefan Kochan of Tarnobrzeg, Adam Latawiec of Gdansk, Ludwik Pawelec of Warsaw. And also by those who only spent the occupation here -- Zbigniew Bączkowski, son of Wiesia Bączkowski, Andrzej Migdałek, and Ewa Dziadek -- children of the schoolteacher Migdałek.

"There will be enough people to testify" -- they say -- "don't you worry, miss, just write your book."

There is also the sister of Karol Liebeskind, though she prefers to remain anonymous. She doesn't want to return to those years, didn't know the Kosińskis; she left Dąbrowa when they arrived. She found out about them from local people, from people with whom she is still in contact. Yet, she always maintains that thanks to them -- thanks to the red partisans, Dąbrowa, the vicinity -- her brother, with "not the best appearance" -- almost managed to survive the occupation -- he was killed literally a few days before the Russians entered, in June 1944.

They tried to forget about him, as in the past they had tried to forget about the "old man." But, it was probably in May 1991, the shocking news was heard that "he had died"! In fact, that he had committed suicide by putting a plastic bag over his head and then drowning himself in a bathtub!

As everyone else, they were at first surprised -- enjoying such prosperity? From the Big World?

And they felt most sorry for the "old man" -- he had tried so hard, had moved heaven and earth, was ready to sign a pact with the devil to save that boy of his, and this is how his son repaid him! Instead of praying for his father to the end of his days!

On the other hand, they were not surprised -- for they remembered how they had once cursed the "old man": "May God repay him in his children!" "May He plague him in his children!"

And they surely uttered this in an evil hour. For why it came true after so many years! God often punishes parents in their children; He punishes the parents in what is most important for them.

There is another explanation. Maybe his conscience was bothering him?

The simple Dąbrowa folks think that, eventually, a person's conscience gets to him; it moves even the worst sinner, such as Judas, who betrayed Jesus to the priests for thirty pieces of silver, which they didn't want to take back. Apparently, neither did the pieces of silver for the *Bird* bring happiness or peace for long.

It's not only a question of the *Bird,* for if that were all, it wouldn't matter! Who

would forever continue to make a fuss over a book?

But during his visits to Poland, his appearances on television, he acted as if they didn't exist, he dissembled, laughed in their faces

Even though in Warsaw he had seen the Warchołs, Madurski, got his letter, so he knew that they were alive, that they were watching him on television; and despite this, he acted as if they didn't exist.

He was in every newspaper, even on Television News, mentioned everyone expect them! He spoke big words about his "ties with his native country," that he "cries only in Polish," but they laughed and said:

"Did you even offer Edward Warchoł a cup of tea? Did you send a word of greeting to old Mrs. Warchoł, who hid you, when she was still living? And to all of Dąbrowa and the vicinity -- you were as silent as the grave!"

He also said how much he was going to do for Poland -- if only in the Kazimierz district of Cracow, which he intended to restore. But they couldn't bear to listen to this.

"Did the people of Kazimierz harbor him? Did cows from Kazimierz feed him?" -- they asked.

And he was everywhere -- in Warsaw, Łódź, Cracow, Kazimierz, Oświęcim. At the Royal Castle, author's meetings, but not in Dąbrowa, where he had survived, even though the village itself went to see him, but how did he receive it? And to make matters worse he lied that he would come, that he would write.

To this day they are still eating bitter fruit.

Mrs. Bogumita Jozwiak recently read somewhere: "He spent his wartime childhood in a world of savagery and violence, among pitiless, ignorant peasants who tried to outdo each other in sadism, debauchery."

And she felt very offended, of course, for it was in Dąbrowa that he had survived, so this referred to them! She and her husband, who was still living then, once even wanted to write to the American embassy, for her husband was an American citizen. In the end, they didn't write, they didn't have the address, and didn't know where to get it. And besides, what was the use? Who would pay any attention to a letter from Dąbrowa peasants?

Adam Latawiec, a native of Wola Rzeczycka, today an engineer living in Gdańsk, and Mr. Andrzej Migdałek, son of the teacher Migdałek, had already written about Kosiński.

"... I assert unequivocally and with full responsibility" -- wrote Adam Latawiec *(Polityka* No. 224/1992) – that "... he lived among us, not a hair of his head was touched, not the least harm came to him."

He was supported by Andrzej Migdałek *(Polityka* No. 10/1993):

"... In his article on Jerzy Kosiński Dave Smith quoted a passage from Jerzy Kosiński's biography -- that at the age of 9 he supposedly lost his speech for 6 years after peasants threw him into a cesspool filled with human excrement.

This is a figment of Jerzy Kosiński's warped mind, for he never lost his speech. He spoke with us in correct Polish, lived with his parents, was never in an orphanage, since liberation found the family in Oqbrowa, from where they later returned to Łódź.

The village harbored the Kosińskis and helped them as much as it was able -- I have many witnesses to this. The village deserves the medal "Just among the Nations of the World," for it saved the writer Jerzy Kosiński from certain death."

Even though *Polityka* printed passages from their letters, nothing changed. Biographers continued to write:

"... Abandoned during the war, thrown among primitive rabble with no feelings, somewhere on the periphery of Polish civilization."

Today no one is any longer surprised that he did not mention them or come to see them. For how could he?

The naked truth is that there were no "borderlands," no boy-wanderer, just loving, affluent parents. No savages -- just people who were simple, perhaps, but decent, who helped as much as they could. No tortures of which he became the symbol; on the contrary -- a rather exceptional fate.

And the "old man"? Maybe it was his doing? Maybe it was on his account? His secret? The price of survival?

Or maybe Jerzy became frightened that Dąbrowa would no longer be their secret?

In Warsaw he had seen ghosts which he preferred to forget about -- the Warchołs, Madurski, perhaps he got his letter. Maybe he had read Migdałek's and Latawiec's letters in *Polityka?*

So maybe he feared that during his next visit to Poland, which had just been announced, they would come "after him," but this time not just the Warchołs and Madurski but all of Dąbrowa, Kępa, Wola?

They would ask him about the "old man" -- why had he run away?

They had also read *The Painted Bird,* and this time they would not let themselves be dismissed and sent away so easily.

Someone would finally notice them, and then he would really be in a fix!

So in the face of all of this, why did he come to Poland at all? Was he tempting fate? He probably thought that they had died, or that they wouldn't dare to come "after him," for how could they -- after such a celebrity? And besides, though to them he was still small or young, he was getting older and maybe something was drawing him back to Poland?

✳ ✳ ✳

They always thought that sooner or later he would stop clowning, stop pretending that they didn't exist. That he would finally visit them, say that *The Painted Bird* is just a "story" and that he had survived thanks to them! And that it would be as on television, which often shows films about Jews who after years come back to visit the places where they survived the occupation. They greet the people, cry, recollect, are happy to be alive, for that is what's most important.

But to the end he remained unyielding.

Even though several people from Dąbrowa swear by all that's holy that this is no "story," that he was here, that they saw him, and that it is he without a doubt! "Little Kusiński"!

During his second visit to Poland, he came late in the evening, when it was already quite dark, in a big black limousine driven by a chauffeur. The car drove very slowly through the entire vicinity a few times -- Dąbrowa, Kępa, Wola. He just looked through the window, observed. Still quite a few wooden prewar cottages, which he perhaps remembered. The bird-fancier Lech's cottage decorated with cages filled with birds. Modest farms, small fields -- these are still poor parts. Wells -

-- cranes -- wooden fences, with benches in front of them. On the country roads -- geese, ducks, sometimes carts.

He did not get out of the limousine; he was probably afraid they would recognize him, come running out. Several people saw him, however, including nearly everyone living where Warchoł's barracks had once stood.

When Karol Liebeskind's sister comes here to visit her brother's grave, she always goes only to the cemetery -- never to where the barracks once stood, where she lived with her parents and brother. Despite the passage of so many years, it is still too painful for her; she is afraid of her reactions, of the memories this place might bring back to her...

But he circled this place a few times, and could it be that it happened here? Maybe it was here that the ghosts finally got to him and from now on no longer let him sleep or live? Tormented him day and night? Took away his reason?

✳ ✳ ✳

Maybe this is enough? They have already said too much about him and hope they won't have new troubles on account of this.

What is more, he's no longer alive, and he died so tragically, so terribly that his death makes one look at him differently -- maybe his conscience did bother him after all?

It's also sad that they can't say anything good about the deceased, but is this their fault? So enough has been said, let him rest in peace.

He is now facing the judgment of God, and so it's not for them to judge him.

The most they can do is to pray for him; after all, he was their parishioner -- he took his First Holy Communion in the church in Wola, and before this Father Sebastianski must have baptized him.

A penitent soul always feels relief after prayer, suffers for a shorter time in purgatory. Of most help is the rosary, especially the second part, the painful, interrupted Station of the Cross:

O my Jesus, forgive us our sins,
preserve us from the fire of hell.
Lead all souls to heaven
and especially help those
who most need Your mercy.

Appendices

Documents from the National Archive in Sandomierz: place of residence certificates of Kosiński and his family (they used the name "Lewinkopf" then) from Gołębicka, Zamkowa and Za Bramką Street.

cz. 6a.　　　1/2/40

KARTA ZAMELDOWANIA
dla przybywających na pobyt czasowy

powiat　　　　　　　　gmina

ul. _Gożlicka_　　　Nr domu _3_　　Nr mieszk. _____

1. Nazwisko _Lewinkopf_

2. Imiona _Mojżesz_

3. Imiona rodziców _Kusyn i Basia_

4. Przybył(a) na pobyt czasowy dn. _31_ m-ca _marca_ 194_1_ r.

u kogo się zatrzymał (a) _u W. Skobla, Sandomier, Gożlicka_

5. Miejsce zamieszkania _Łódź, gdańska 77_

(za miejsce zamieszkania uważa się miejsce gdzie dana osoba figuruje w rejestrze mieszkańców, czyli gdzie jest po raz ostatni na stałe meldowana)

6. Urodził (a) się dn. _18_ m-ca _październik_ 18_91_ r.

w _ul. J. Lipińskiego, Sandomier, Zamk. 8_

127

1/2/40   W z ó r   Nr   3/V

KARTA ZAMELDOWANIA
dla przybywających na pobyt czasowy

powiat   gmina   miejscowość lub Komisariat P. P.

ul. *Za bramka* .... Nr domu *4* .. Nr mieszk. ....

1. Nazwisko *Lewinkopf*

2. Imiona *Wojciech*

3. Imiona rodziców *Wacyn i Basia*

4. Przybył(a) na pobyt czasowy dn. *16* m-ca *sierpnia 1942* r.

   u kogo się zatrzymał(a) *w mieszkaniu własnym*

5. Miejsce zamieszkania *Sandomierz, Za bramka 4*

6. Wiek *51 lat*

7. Osoby towarzyszące:

   a) żona *Elżbieta*

   b) ojciec ....

   c) matka ....

   d) dzieci do lat 18 *Jerzy - Nikodem*

   ....

128

m. 40   1/2/40

KARTA ZAMELDOWANIA
dla przybywających na pobyt czasowy

powiat   gmina

ul. *Tyszicka*   Nr domu *3*   Nr mieszk.

1. Nazwisko *Lewinkopf*

2. Imiona *Elżbieta*

3. Imiona rodziców *Majer i Sura*

4. Przybył(a) na pobyt czasowy dn. *31* m-ca *marca* 194 *1* r.

u kogo się zatrzymał (a) *W. Skobel, Sandomierz Tyszicka 3*

5. Miejsce zamieszkania

Łódź, Gdańska 74

*(za miejsce zamieszkania uważa się miejsce gdzie dana osoba figuruje
w rejestrze mieszkańców, czyli gdzie jest po raz ostatni na stałe
meldowana)*

6. Urodził (a) się dn. *6* m-ca *stycznia* 1.8 *99* r.

w *J. Lipińskiego Sandomierz Zamkowa 8*

1/2/40

KARTA ZAMELDOWANIA
dla przybywających na pobyt czasowy

powiat   gmina

ul. *Go Tybicka*   Nr domu *3*   Nr mieszk.

1. Nazwisko *Levinkopf*

2. Imiona *Jerzy Nikodem*

3. Imiona rodziców *Mojżesz i Elżbieta*

4. Przybył(a) na pobyt czasowy dn. *31* m-ca *marca* 1941 r.

u kogo się zatrzymał (a) *Go Tybicka*

5. Miejsce zamieszkania *Łódź, Gdańska 74*

(za miejsce zamieszkania uważa się miejsce gdzie dana osoba figuruje w rejestrze mieszkańców, czyli gdzie jest po raz ostatni na stałe meldowana)

6. Urodził (a) się dn. *17* m-ca *wrzesień* w *Łodzi* 1933 r.

130

Printed in Great Britain
by Amazon